Consulting Pupils

What's in it for schools?

The *What's in it for schools?* series aims to make educational policy issues relevant to practitioners. Each book in the series focuses on a major educational issue. The authors set the issue in context, look at how it impacts on the daily lives of schools and teachers, and raise key questions. The books are grounded in sound theory, recent research evidence and best practice, and will make an excellent addition to any staffroom bookshelf.

Consulting Pupils considers the potential benefits and implications of talking to pupils about teaching and learning in school, exploring its impact at different levels. Key issues included are:

- The importance of engaging young learners in a focused dialogue about learning.
- The role of pupil consultation in helping schools to develop new directions for improvement.
- The wider implications of pupil consultation and participation in teaching the principles of citizenship and democracy.

Through examples of pupil consultation initiatives in primary and secondary schools, the authors demonstrate how an agenda for change based on pupils' perspectives on teaching and learning can be used to improve classroom practice.

This book will be a valuable resource for practitioners, students and researchers interested in exploring pupils' perspectives on teaching and learning.

Julia Flutter is Research Associate and **Jean Rudduck** is Professor of Education, both at the School of Education, University of Cambridge.

What's in it for schools?

Edited by Kate Myers and John MacBeath

Consulting Pupils

What's in it for schools?

Julia Flutter
Jean Rudduck

RoutledgeFalmer
Taylor & Francis Group

LONDON AND NEW YORK

First published 2004
by RoutledgeFalmer
11 New Fetter Lane, London EC4P 4EE

Simultaneously published in the USA and Canada
by RoutledgeFalmer
29 West 35th Street, New York, NY 10001

RoutledgeFalmer is an imprint of the Taylor & Francis Group

© 2004 Julia Flutter & Jean Rudduck

Typeset in Baskerville by Graphicraft Limited, Hong Kong
Printed and bound in Great Britain by TJ International Limited, Padstow, Cornwall

British Library Cataloguing in Publication Data
A catalogue record for this book is available from the British Library

Library of Congress Cataloging in Publication Data
   Flutter, Julia.
      Consulting pupils : what's in it for schools? / Julia Flutter and
   Jean Rudduck.
         p. cm. – (What's in it for schools?)
      Includes bibliographical references.
      1. Teacher-student relationships–Great Britain–Case studies.   2. Student
   participation in administration–Great Britain–Case studies.   3. Communication
   in education–Great Britain–Case studies. I. Rudduck, Jean. II. Title. III. Series.
   LB1033.F58 2004
   371.102′3–dc22

                                                                    2003018472

ISBN 0-415-26304-2 (hbk)
ISBN 0-415-26305-0 (pbk)

Contents

List of figures and tables

Acknowledgements

This book is based on research with schools over the past ten years and we would like to thank all those who have given so much time and energy in working on these projects with us. We are always impressed with the dedicated professionalism of the teachers who take part in our research – to put in extra hours at the end of long days spent in the classroom is a tremendous feat and a testimony of their commitment to young learners. We have also been deeply impressed with the young people who have spoken to us during these projects. Their willingness to engage in serious and frank conversations about the things that matter to them – their learning, their futures, their experiences – is an eloquent defence against the media's charge of apathy in young people today.

Much of the data in this book was gathered during the project, Consulting Pupils about Teaching and Learning, one of four research projects in Phase 1 of the Economic and Social Research Council's Teaching and Learning Research Programme. We are very grateful to the Economic and Social Research Council for providing this opportunity for us to extend our work on pupil consultation and for the invaluable support of Professor Andrew Pollard (the Programme Director) and his team.

We would also like to thank our Series Editors, John MacBeath and Kate Myers, for their guidance and gentle chivvying which have helped to get this book (finally!) onto the bookshelves.

Series editors' preface

Kate Myers and John MacBeath

Series introduction

There is a concerted move to raise standards in the public education system. The aim is laudable. Few people would disagree with it. However, there is no clear agreement about what we mean by 'standards'. Do we mean attainment or achievement more broadly defined, for example, and how we are to raise whatever it is we agree needs raising?

At the same time, there appears to be an increasing trend towards approaching changes in education through a controlling, rational and technical framework. This framework tends to concentrate on educational content and delivery and ignores the human-resource perspective and the complexity of how human beings live, work and interact with one another. It overemphasizes linearity and pays insufficient attention to how people respond to change and either support or subvert it.

Recent government initiatives, including the National Curriculum, OFSTED school and LEA inspections, assessment procedures, league tables, target-setting, literacy and numeracy hours, and performance management have endorsed this framework. On occasions this has been less to do with the content of 'reforms' than the process of implementation – that is, doing it 'to' rather than 'with' the teaching profession. Teachers are frequently treated as the problem rather than part of the solution, with the consequence that many feel disillusioned, demoralised and disempowered. Critics of the *top-down* approach are often seen as lacking rigour, complacent about standards, and uninterested in raising achievement.

We want to edit this series because we believe that you can be passionate about public education, about raising achievement, about ensuring that all pupils are entitled to the best possible education that society is able to provide – whatever their race, sex or class. We also believe that achieving this is not a simple matter of common sense or of the appliance of science – it is more complex than that. Most of all, we see the teaching profession as an important part of the solution to finding ways through these complexities.

What's in it for schools? is a series that will make educational policy issues relevant to practitioners. Each book in the series focuses on a major educational issue and raises key questions, such as:

- Can inspection be beneficial to schools?
- How can assessment procedures help pupils learn?
- How can school self-evaluation improve teaching and learning?
- What impact does leadership in the school have in the classroom?
- How can school improvement become classroom improvement?

The books are grounded in sound theory, recent research evidence and best practice, and aim to:

- help you to make meaning personally and professionally from knowledge in a given field
- help you to seek out practical applications of an area of knowledge for classrooms and schools
- help those of you who want to research the field in greater depth, by providing key sources with accessible summaries and recommendations.

In addition, each book identifies key issues and questions for reflection or further discussion, enabling schools to use the books as a resource for whole-school staff development.

We hope that the books in this series will show you that there are ways of raising achievement that can take account of how schools grow and develop and how teachers work and interact with one another. *What's in it for schools?* – a great deal, we think!

Preface

Asking consumers what they think about a service or product has become common practice in recent years. Politicians, public service providers and companies have been quick to recognise the value of consultation because it not only makes consumers feel that they matter but also provides valuable information for tailoring services (or manifestos) to suit consumers (or voters) at large. In education, providers and policy makers have been slower to realise the potential of consulting 'consumers'. The drive for school improvement, however, has prompted schools to look for new directions in planning for change, and interest in what pupils have to say about teaching and learning has grown in response to these endeavours.

This book explores how – and why – schools have been developing strategies for pupil consultation and participation. In Chapter 1 we look at the different ways in which pupils, teachers and schools can benefit from these strategies. Chapter 2 focuses on methodological dimensions of consultation and participation and, using a wide range of real-life examples, it considers the issues that schools need to think about before introducing these strategies. The key themes emerging from our research on pupils' perspectives are presented in Chapter 3 to illustrate the kinds of insight that can be gained through consulting pupils. The concluding section discusses the transformational potential of the pupil voice movement for the future of schools.

Our principal aim in writing this book has been to show what pupil consultation and participation strategies can do for schools and we hope that it will encourage others to try out these ideas in their own practice.

Note: In this book we have generally used the word 'pupils' to describe children and young people in schools. We realise that some readers might prefer us to use the word 'students' but, as this more commonly refers to learners in post-compulsory education than to learners in schools in the UK, we wanted to avoid possible confusion.

1 Pupil consultation as a key to improving teaching and learning

Teachers and pupils today might be forgiven for wondering whether, rather than entering a place of learning every working day, they are, in fact, stepping into a football stadium. Surrounded by an eager crowd of politicians, parents and employers, they are keenly aware that what happens inside the classroom is being watched, scrutinised, evaluated and publicly debated. 'Targets' and 'goals', 'performance' and 'league tables' are the banners waved enthusiastically by education policy makers and the media and, just like football teams, teachers and pupils find their performances vilified when public expectations do not seem to have been met. It is easy to see how this model has infiltrated education: through government schemes that aim to recognise and reward the successful, through systems of inspection and measurement designed to pressure relentlessly for 'higher scores' and through the establishment of a competitive structure where some schools find themselves singled out as 'failing'. The public have been captivated by the language and style of this winner-takes-all culture but, while notions of 'competition', 'improvement' and 'reward' are in themselves worthwhile and appropriate within certain contexts, it must be recognised that learning is far more important, complex and demanding than any game and, as a society, we cannot afford to relegate any young person to failure.

While it is clear that much remains to be done to ensure that our educational system matches up to the demands of the twenty-first century, this political drive for higher standards and greater accountability has not necessarily supported schools effectively in meeting the challenges and, as national statistics continue to confirm, too many young people leave school without the qualifications and skills they need for successful and fulfilling adult lives.

Consulting pupils: a new direction for school improvement?

If the constant barrage of change and reform in education, directed by successive governments, has not succeeded in resolving many of the pervasive problems in education, then where else can we look to find solutions? The answer is, perhaps, an obvious but often over-looked one: to find new directions for improving schools we must take as our starting point the classroom itself and explore teaching and learning through the eyes of those most closely involved – teachers and young learners. Their guidance can be used to direct our atten-tion to the issues that need to be given priority in planning improve-ment. Only in this way will teachers be enabled to develop new strategies based on a deeper knowledge and firmer understanding of the complex processes of teaching and learning.

Where the objective of the investigation is to improve teaching and learning, then it is only the testimony of pupils and teachers them-selves that can provide essential, first-hand evidence. Of course, other 'expert witnesses' from a range of fields may also make important contributions to the consultation but, unlike teachers and pupils, these experts cannot offer perspectives based on direct experience. When we invite teachers and pupils to give us their accounts of teaching and learning, we are interested in more than 'factual' testimony in the legal sense because we also want to discover more about their percep-tions of, and attitudes towards, their experiences in classrooms and schools. Whilst these perceptions might not constitute admissible evidence in a court of law, in the context of an investigation aimed at improving teaching and learning, such evidence is a vital resource. It allows us to identify the things that teachers and young learners consider important and that make a difference to pupils' opportunities for successful learning.

Until fairly recently, pupils were rarely invited to bring their perspect-ives on teaching and learning into the development frame. Evidence has been drawn from observational studies, ethnographies, experiments and action research interventions but the researchers' perspectives have defined the boundaries of what counts as evidence. Too often, although with some very notable exceptions (for example, Martyn Hammersley, Linda Measor and Peter Woods' pioneering research on pupils' experiences of schooling), research has concentrated on looking in from the outside and has not focused on participants' conceptions of teaching and learning; yet it is these conceptions that form the 'realities' of pupils' and teachers' working lives and understanding these realities is essential to our objective of making teaching and learning more effective.

However, although we are proposing that pupils' perspectives are worthy of attention, we do not suggest that undue weight should be given to them. We would agree with Nixon and his colleagues who have pointed out that 'The pupil testimony is not privileged as more "true" than the accounts of teachers and advisers, but it provides a crucial element still too often overlooked' (1996: 270). We also share the concern expressed by American researcher Sonia Nieto, who cautions that taking account of the pupil perspective 'is not meant to suggest that their ideas should be the final and conclusive word in how schools need to change'; and that to place too great an emphasis on their contribution is 'to accept a romantic view of students that is just as partial and condescending as excluding them completely from the discussions' (Nieto, 1994: 398). We are not proposing that pupils should dictate how schools are run but our research leads us to believe that practitioners and schools can benefit from tuning into pupils' perspectives.

Investigating pupils' perceptions and attitudes is not a new idea in education research but some earlier researchers adopted the view that pupils are sources of data whose behaviour and responses should simply be studied, measured and recorded. As Roche points out, there are signs that this is changing:

> Increasingly a new kind of work with and writing on children is being done. There is much literature which explores how children and young people see the world, their values and priorities and the ways in which they feel themselves marginalised . . .
>
> (Roche, 1999: 477)

Until recently there have been relatively few attempts to involve pupils as active participants in classroom-based research investigations and school improvement initiatives. However, as Gross argues, the benefits in adopting this type of collaborative approach are plain: 'Ongoing collaboration with students helps determine direction and develop emphases for specific changes toward an improved teaching–learning situation' (1997: 80). In the following section we consider the 'gridline' of questions that will enable us to gain a clearer picture of pupils' perspectives on teaching and learning in school.

A question of learning

Asking questions is, of course, a familiar part of classroom life and teachers use the technique of asking questions in a variety of ways during lessons. They may, for example, ask a question to check whether pupils have understood instructions or to prompt pupils' thinking about problems and possible solutions. Pupils are also likely to ask teachers questions, perhaps to gain more information about what they are supposed to do or to request help in understanding something they have not yet grasped. But there are some important questions that, somewhat surprisingly, are rarely heard in the classroom and these are questions concerning the learning process itself. Consider for a moment the following questions:

- How do you learn best?
- What helps you to learn?
- What gets in the way of your learning?
- Why do you find it more difficult to learn certain things?
- Do you learn better through particular styles of teaching?
- What encourages you to work harder at your learning?
- How do you know if you have succeeded in learning something?

Some of these questions are quite difficult to answer and need to be explored through discussion where different perspectives are brought into play. Although the issues and topics under investigation are likely to vary according to the focus of the enquiry or the school's particular interests or concerns, pupil consultation is principally about gathering information to help illuminate such questions.

For some years we have been working on investigations that explore what pupils have to say about teaching and learning and the conditions of learning in their schools. Our research has also looked at how schools have developed different kinds of strategies based on pupil consultation. These initiatives have highlighted some of the potential benefits that these processes can offer to teachers and schools. But what do we mean when we refer to these two terms, 'pupil consultation' and 'pupil participation'?

What do we mean by 'pupil consultation'?

Consultation is defined as 'the action of taking counsel together; deliberation or conference' and this notion of 'taking counsel' suggests that the parties involved in the consultation process have been invited to contribute because they have relevant and important views and information to share. Pupil consultation, therefore, rests on the principle that pupils can bring something worthwhile to discussions about schooling. The term can be applied to any research or development strategy or research approach that invites pupils to talk about their experiences as learners in school. Pupil consultation is nested within the broader principle of pupil participation.

What do we mean by 'pupil participation'?

The principle of pupil participation requires that pupils should be given an active and direct involvement in school matters, at some level. Although all pupils 'participate' in the basic sense that they attend a school, receive teaching instruction and have their name on a register, the term 'pupil participation' suggests inclusion, or membership, of a community, in which pupils are valued and respected contributors. The principles of democracy and citizenship are also linked with the notion of pupil participation, as Gerison Lansdown suggests:

> Participation can be defined as the process of sharing in decisions which affect one's life and the life of the community in which one lives . . . In the field of education in this country there is a great deal of discussion about the need to teach children responsibility, citizenship and respect for others, but these skills and attitudes are not ones which can be acquired merely through the taught curriculum. The understanding, competence and commitment to

democratic participation can only be achieved through practice and experience.

(1995: 17)

Researching pupils' perspectives

When we are looking for answers to the problems affecting our society we often fail to recognise that *how things are* is often less important than *how people think* – or perceive – things are. In other words, people's conceptions of the world around them are profoundly significant, both to themselves and to others, because it is these perceived 'realities' that give shape and meaning to people's lives and actions. Indeed, as Thomas and Thomas proposed, 'If men define situations as real, they are real in their consequences' (1928: 572). Recognition of this key point has profound implications for our endeavours to improve what happens in schools for, unless we look at the experiences of teaching and learning through the eyes of young learners, we, like Cervantes' Don Quixote, may be in some danger of tilting at windmills. We may be wasting our time and energy wrangling with issues that may, from an outside perspective, appear to be real, 'solid' concerns but which are, in fact, illusions. As Michael Apple suggests: '. . . to understand schools one must go beyond what educational practitioners and theorists *think* is going on . . .' ([1979] 1990: 141, our emphasis). The issues currently attracting policy makers' and media attention – such as truancy, male underachievement and classroom discipline – may look rather different when viewed through the lens of pupil perspectives. There has, for example, been much debate about why boys are underachieving but our pupil data suggest that factors influencing pupil achievement are more complex than this simple question may at first suggest. Although more boys than girls appear to be affected, the problem of underachievement may not be wholly ascribed to the condition of 'being male' as some commentators have argued. We may gain a deeper understanding of these problems and underlying factors if we address a broader set of questions with all young learners:

- How can lessons be made more engaging?
- Do pupils feel that what they are learning is relevant and important?

• Are schools providing conditions for learning that enable all learners to succeed?

Our research with primary and secondary schools across the UK has demonstrated that pupils of all ages can show a remarkable capacity to discuss their learning in a considered and insightful way, although they may not always be able to articulate their ideas in the formal language of education. We have also observed that, in some cases, the opportunity to participate in a learning-focused dialogue may help to improve pupils' attitudes towards teachers and schools. There is also evidence to suggest that it may also have a beneficial effect on pupils' performance (for example, see Watkins, 2001). But why should this process of dialogue – of thinking and talking about learning – affect pupils' progress? Feedback from teachers on pupil consultation strategies offers a partial answer to this question. Teachers have reported that listening to what pupils say has helped them to understand how pupils learn most effectively and led to them reconsider, and make changes to, aspects of their own teaching practice:

> Encouraging pupils to explicitly engage in [such] a self-questioning exercise helps them to begin to think about and take control of their own learning. It can also provide the teacher with the valuable information needed for differentiating work and developing effective support activities for individual learners who may have special needs.
>
> (Doran and Cameron, 1995: 17)

As some of the school profiles presented in this book suggest, where teachers have made improvements to their practice, based on information drawn from pupil consultation, they have reported positive outcomes in terms of pupils' attitudes and behaviour and, in some cases, also of their performance.

However, another, rather different, answer lies in the potential impact on young learners themselves, as observed by Mike Jelly and colleagues, who consulted pupils as part of their research with special needs schools. These researchers found clear evidence that consulting young learners about their learning enhanced self-esteem and confidence, promoted stronger engagement and motivation to learn and encouraged pupils to become more active members of the school community (Jelly *et al.*, 2000). As pupil consultation becomes used more widely, and the impact of these initiatives is monitored and evaluated, there is increasing evidence of a range of positive outcomes for pupils, for teachers and for schools.

Improving learning

Giving young learners opportunities to think and talk about aspects of teaching and learning can have a direct impact on pupils' metacognitive development and on their understanding of how they learn (see, for example, Pramling, 1990, Quicke, 1994). Learning-focused dialogue is particularly useful both as a strategy for identifying pupils' difficulties with aspects of their learning and as a way of developing their capacity to reflect on and improve their learning. The term 'metacognition' (Nisbet and Schucksmith, 1986) refers to the ability to think about one's own thinking and learning processes. As McCallum *et al.* point out, this capacity lies at the heart of effective learning:

> The importance of the learner's role is also supported by one of the concepts that has emerged from work in psychology and cognitive science, that of metacognition. Good learners monitor their learning using strategies which hinge on self-questioning, in order to get the purpose of learning clear, searching for connections and conflicts with what is already known. Thus, the pupil's active engagement in the learning process is a key element in these models of learning.
>
> (McCallum *et al.*, 2000: 276)

Researchers Doran and Cameron have also found evidence to suggest that a learning-focused dialogue can have a lasting impact on pupils' thinking skills. They argued that such dialogue is an essential prerequisite for improving learning in the classroom:

> The most promising medium for encouraging the growth of these superordinate and previously neglected components of learning success, is likely to involve a teacher–learner dialogue which seeks

to develop a shared perspective of the learning process . . . When such a learning dialogue is in place, pupils will begin to gain a sense of competency and self worth, not through cajoling or threatening, but by recognising and responding to the evidence of their own efforts and achievements. Such a motivational force would propel the learning throughout life dynamic required for personal and professional development in the constantly changing context of the next decades.

(Doran and Cameron, 1995: 22)

Research carried out by Black *et al.* (2002) suggests that there is a need for teachers to focus more closely on classroom dialogue and to develop classroom strategies that encourage pupils to think and talk about their learning. In particular, Black and his colleagues have iden-tified the importance of assessment practices – which they describe as 'assessment *for* learning' – that provide effective support for pupils' learning:

Assessment for learning is any assessment for which the first pri-ority in its design and practice is to serve the purpose of pupils' learning. It thus differs from assessment designed primarily to serve the purposes of accountability, or of ranking, or of certifying competence.

(Black *et al.*, 2002: 1)

The following example, from our Effective Learning Project (see Appendix 3) illustrates how pupil consultation can be used to examine pupils' understandings of key aspects of teaching and learning. Teachers at a large comprehensive secondary school in Cambridgeshire decided to explore pupils' perspectives on 'What makes a piece of work good'. They were concerned that pupils did not fully understand what was expected of them. Analysis of the school's interview and questionnaire data suggested that although pupils regarded marks and teacher com-ments as important indicators of achievement and progress, there was confusion about the marking system and many pupils had little idea about improving the quality of their work. Through this initiative the school was able to develop new assessment processes that gave more detailed guidance to pupils about their performance and provided clearer advice on how to improve the standard of their work in different subject areas.

Data from the Effective Learning Project also revealed how assessment played a key role in shaping pupils' identities as learners and alerted teachers to the importance of giving feedback in ways that were sensitive and supportive to the needs of all young learners. It is widely recognised that pupils who are less confident in their abilities as learners are particularly vulnerable to loss of motivation when continually faced with poor results and negative feedback (Dweck, 1986). Evidence gathered in our pupil consultation projects confirms the profound impact that frequent negative feedback can have on attitudes and self-esteem. However, we also noted that confidence and engagement with learning could be restored, in some cases, if pupils were given opportunities to experience successes in their learning and if they were supported in developing more positive self-images. These two extracts from our interviews with two Year 11 boys (15–16-year-olds) who were studying in a student support unit indicate that supportive assessment procedures can make a difference to pupils' engagement with learning:

> If, you know, instead of a teacher saying 'Oh that's not good enough! Do it again because you've got one word wrong', you've actually got a teacher saying to you, 'That was a very imaginative, well-written piece of work' – that's like, well, a reward in a way. (Y11 boy)

> Before, a lot of teachers just used to think I was useless and I would never try my best whereas now they like acknowledge that I am trying my best and that does make it a lot easier to get on with work and motivates you to do things. (Y11 boy)

However, the potential of thinking and talking about learning for improving pupils' learning lies not only in investigating the things that help or hinder but also in the positive impact that engaging in dialogue can have on pupils' understanding of how they learn. There are, of course, many conflicting priorities absorbing teachers' time but, as Charlton points out, there is a need to recognise that making time to talk with pupils about learning can reap tremendous rewards:

Active listening (in an interpersonal context) is rarely given the recognition and time it deserves in classrooms and schools, or elsewhere . . . Children stand to derive much benefit from being listened to: their academic success can be improved, their personal problems can be reduced, their self-esteem and motivation can be enhanced.

(Charlton, 1996a: 62)

As well as talking about learning, research has demonstrated that giving pupils opportunities to participate more actively in the learning process is important. Many studies have indicated the potential benefits of initiatives focused on increasing pupil involvement in various ways. For example, Schweinhart and Weikart's longitudinal study (1993) of the American 'High/Scope' noted the long-term positive impact of pupils' participation in planning, executing and reviewing their learning. A further example is Harpfield Primary School's initiative with Year 5 (9–10-year-olds) and Year 6 (10–11-year-olds) pupils (see Profile 5, Chapter 2) which illustrates how involving pupils in making decisions about teaching activities can encourage greater independence in learning. There is also clear evidence that pupil participation in assessment, whether in self-assessment or peer assessment strategies, can provide an effective way of helping pupils to understand how to improve their work (Roller, 1999).

Although pupil consultation and pupil participation appear to have some beneficial effect on individual pupil performance, it is often difficult to quantify the extent to which these strategies make an impact because they represent only one dimension of the context of learning in school; many other factors are also likely to have a bearing on achievement. We will return to consider some of these issues in Chapter 3 where we explore pupils' perspectives on things that support their learning.

Improving teaching

Learning is sometimes seen happening inside 'the black box' – as an individual and somewhat mysterious process of absorbing information and acquiring skills – but it is, of course, a social process. It is usually dependent on interaction with others and is given its shape and meaning by the community in which it occurs. Involving pupils in discussions about teaching and learning represents a recognition of the social nature of learning and helps us to look at more than one isolated piece in the jigsaw of education. Looking at teaching and learning from the pupil perspective can therefore provide teachers with insights into the complex factors affecting pupils' progress.

The information gleaned from pupil consultation data offers a valuable resource for teachers' professional development. The idea of pupil consultation as a tool for informing practice has been taken up by researchers Cooper and Hyland who have looked at pupils' perspectives on initial teacher training. They concluded that

> Matters of principle and pragmatism meet when it is recognized that pupils can actively contribute to teachers' developing skills and professional knowledge. The practical justification for enquiring into pupils' perspectives is that their ideas on their school experience are directly relevant to developing more effective teaching.
>
> (Cooper and Hyland, 2000: 22)

The potential of pupil consultation as a strategy for improving teaching also extends to more experienced practitioners for, as Cullingford suggests, pupils' perspectives can help teachers to reflect on their practice, look at ways of improving some aspects of their teaching and develop new ideas:

> Children reveal that they have the articulate-ness and honesty to analyse what they experience. They show consistent judgment and evidence for what they are saying. Their views deserve to be taken into account because they know better than anyone which teaching and learning styles are successful, which techniques of learning bring the best out of them and what the ethos of the school consists of . . . listening to children makes us consider some of the habits we have taken for granted.
>
> (Cullingford, 1991: 2)

One of the more common uses of pupil consultation has been as a means for teachers to gather feedback from pupils on the effectiveness of different aspects of practice. Although this 'consumer survey' style of pupil consultation can be useful for individual teachers, there are advantages in extending the process. In some other countries, schools have made more extensive use of pupil evaluation: for example, in Vienna, schools invite pupils to comment on the quality of teaching at the end of each term as part of the school review process.

When adopted as a school-wide process, approaches involving pupil consultation and participation can help to create more positive pupil–teacher relationships. At the outset, both teachers and learners may have some reservations and concerns but, once their fears are allayed, the process can lead pupils and teachers to regard each other in a new light. Indeed, pupil consultation strategies may, in some settings, encourage pupils and teachers to see teaching and learning as more of a 'joint endeavour': as one secondary teacher commented, 'It's not about students picking holes in teachers, it's about achieving together.' Pupils who have taken part in consultation projects have also described how these experiences have altered their perceptions of teachers as individuals. Here, younger pupils from Wheatcroft Primary School proclaim the benefits of consultation:

> With the help of teachers and children working together we are making the school a better place. (Patrick, Y4)

> It's nice to know that some teachers want to know how we feel about learning ... I think it is important that the children and teachers have a good relationship – it makes working much easier. (Nicola, Y6)

> The teachers we have are very kind and nice to us all. The children are allowed a say in almost everything. I think that teachers and children have a very good working relationship and I think this is developing very well. (Hannah, Y6)

As well as influencing the character of social relationships within schools and classrooms, pupil consultation allows schools to identify issues that need to be given closer attention. Of course, what pupils say will sometimes raise unexpected issues for teachers who may be unaware of some of the things that concern pupils or things that they attach most importance to. For example, primary and secondary teachers working on the Effective Learning Project consulted pupils about learning environments and were intrigued to discover a range of things that pupils mentioned as having an effect on their learning. Among the things that pupils identified were classroom layout and seating arrangements; problems with lighting and acoustics; the importance of having informative and attractive displays and the need for better access to resources. They also explained how aesthetic aspects of the environment affected their feelings about working in particular rooms and areas. Teachers found these findings useful and were able to plan some changes in their classrooms: for example, by using more wall displays and by experimenting with different seating arrangements. In one secondary school, pupils were consulted about plans for refurbishing some areas of the school. Consulting pupils is a good way of finding out 'what works' in the classroom. For example, in one primary school pupils were asked to think about ways of learning that they found most helpful and interesting. As a consequence of this feedback from pupils, teachers introduced more group work and activities using information technology across the curriculum.

Improving schools

Traditionally, the pupil's role within school has been a somewhat passive one, with pupils regarded as 'consumers', or even as 'products', of educational provision rather than as active participants in a learning community. This traditional role is now beginning to change. As James suggests, conferring opportunities for active agency can have a transforming effect on pupils and, ultimately, on schools themselves: '. . . inviting the young to be responsible persons, the young behave responsibly and the whole character of the school society changes' (1968: 68). In asking pupils for their views on school matters they are also being invited to participate, at some level, in the decision-making processes of their school and this participation can have a positive impact on their attitudes and behaviour.

The Economic and Social Research Council/Teaching and Learning Research Programme (ESRC/TLRP) Project, Consulting Pupils about Teaching and Learning (see Appendix 3), has been working closely with schools across the country, exploring how pupil consultation and pupil participation strategies have been developed and how they have contributed to school improvement. Among the schools that took part were some with a long track record of pupil involvement and others that were just starting out. It is interesting to note the reasons why schools initially decided to introduce pupil consultation and participation initiatives and to look at the different paths they have taken. Some schools began their work in response to specific concerns (such as high levels of pupil disengagement with learning, particularly among boys), while others took a broader interest in the notion of pupil voice and saw pupil consultation and pupil participation strategies as contributing to the development of a more positive learning and inclusive culture within the school.

Once the idea of pupil consultation and participation is established in a school, it may evolve in many different ways. Sometimes it will build out from a small group and one teacher to involve more teachers and pupils. This may, in turn, lead to a transformation in school ethos and structure. In others, the initiative may be top-down. Where the innovation is linked to the enthusiasm of a minority, it may not be sustained if some of these teachers leave the school.

The 'ladder' diagram (see Figure 1.1) outlines the routes that pupil participation initiatives in schools may follow, describing increasing levels of involvement for pupils from the basis of 'non-participation' to the highest stage of fully active participation. Data from our Network Project suggest that some schools, which started out on a narrowly focused agenda, have subsequently moved on to a higher 'rung' on the ladder of pupil participation as they recognised the power of pupil voice. We have come across only a few schools who seem to have reached the highest rung of the ladder; but many of our Network Project schools have told us about initiatives which appear to fit the descriptions of rungs 1 and 2, and, as these initiatives evolve and expand, we may see more schools attaining rungs 3 and 4.

In some cases, pupils have been given opportunities to set the agenda of enquiry, to take on roles as researchers or co-researchers and to support teachers in monitoring and evaluating outcomes of new initiatives. In other schools the brief of the school councils has been broadened to include discussion of pedagogical issues so that, rather than pursuing the more traditional – though important – agenda of uniforms, vending machines and lockers, they have begun to open up aspects of teaching and learning. There are several examples of school councils

4. pupils as fully active participants and co-researchers
pupils and teachers jointly initiate enquiry; pupils play an active role in decision making; together with teachers, they plan action in the light of data and review impact of the intervention

3. pupils as researchers
pupils are involved in enquiry and have an active role in decision making; there will be feedback and discussion with pupils regarding findings drawn from the data

2. pupils as active participants
teachers initiate enquiry and interpret the data but pupils are taking some role in decision making; there is likely to be some feedback to pupils on the findings drawn from the data

1. listening to pupils
pupils are a source of data; teachers respond to data but pupils are not involved in discussion of findings; there may be no feedback to pupils; teachers act on the data

0. pupils not consulted
there is no element of pupil participation or pupil consultation within the school

Figure 1.1 The ladder of pupil participation

Source: Based on the Ladder of children's participation in decision-making, in Hart, 1997.

setting up sub-committees to explore issues identified by teachers and pupils (see, for example, Profile 13: Hastingsbury Upper School and Community College) and give feedback to teaching staff. But confidence in the process has to be built up step by step:

We have had a student council, but up until now students have not had a voice in the area of curriculum development . . . Our students have shown themselves to be capable of conducting research with integrity and commitment and this has resulted in their views being seen as important and respected.

(Secondary school teacher)

Teachers at this school have found that pupils generally responded to the initiative with enthusiasm and that most were genuinely construct-ive in their comments.

Whilst it is difficult to quantify the impact of pupil consultation and extended participation on attitudes and performance, teachers and pupils have said that they found these approaches worthwhile. The testimony of a pupil-researcher at Sharnbrook Upper School, which has a long tradition of listening to the pupil voice, describes the strength of the contribution that pupil consultation can make:

As my involvement in the project continued I came to realise more and more that every student is a valued member of the school community, and that how they feel about it does matter. This knowledge not only had a profound effect on a personal level for myself and the other students involved in the project, but also, on a school-wide level, it encourages students to be honest with the school. The research projects undertaken provided the student body with another opportunity to express their opinion, in the knowledge that it would be taken seriously. This kind of know-ledge creates an ethos of respect in the establishment . . .

(Crane, 2001: 54)

Further evidence is offered in a report by the Community Service Volunteers organisation which looked at the impact of citizenship education: the study found evidence suggesting that pupil participa-tion initiatives can increase pupils' motivation, improve attendance and promote better pupil–teacher relationships (CSV, 2002).

The implementation of the Citizenship Education curriculum in England and Wales has led to a resurgence of interest in the school council as a mechanism for introducing principles of democracy. The NSPCC's recent survey on school councils in England reports that most secondary schools have representative school councils and an increasing number of primary schools either have a school council or are intending to set one up in the future (Baginsky and Hannam, 1999). School Councils UK, an organisation supporting school council initiatives, has also seen a rising demand for its training and resources for schools (for details of resources produced by School Councils UK see the 'Recommended Reading' section). In many schools the school council role is limited to discussion of pupils' concerns about facilities, uniforms and rules but there is evidence that schools are willing to adopt innovative approaches. Hannam (1999) cites examples of school councils in English schools which have been involved in interviewing applicants for teaching posts, reviewing teaching and learning strategies and discussing curriculum content. Although these are positive signs, the UK appears to lag behind some other European countries in its promotion of school councils: in Norway, for example, it is a legal requirement for schools to establish school councils for pupils to discuss serious matters concerning learning and assessment.

Another important dimension of approaches based on consultation and participation is that they not only permit pupils to experience and enact democratic principles but also give pupils opportunities to acquire the knowledge and skills necessary for taking an active role in a democratic society in later life. Hart suggests: 'Only through direct participation can children develop a genuine appreciation of democracy and a sense of their own competence and responsibility to participate' (1997: 3). Hart's view is echoed in a comment by a young person taking part in a national research project exploring young people's views of their lives and on the society in which they live: 'Teachers need to understand they are preparing you for the world not just teaching you a subject' (National Children's Bureau, 1998: 20).

Preparing young people to take more active roles as citizens is increasingly being recognised as worthwhile and important outside school. Schemes for children and young people's participation in youth councils, local council consultation schemes and young parliament initiatives are becoming increasingly popular (Wade *et al.*, 2001). However, within schools there has been some hesitation about pupils taking on such responsibilities. In schools in other European countries democratic systems of pupil involvement have been in place for many years:

for example, in Denmark the guidelines for the national curriculum should be implemented through negotiation with both teachers and pupils. However, a recent study by Kerr *et al.* (2002) carried out in 28 countries, including the UK, found that only one quarter of students were encouraged to voice their opinions about schooling. The report concluded:

> Schools that model democratic values and practices by encouraging students to discuss issues in the classroom and take an active role in the life of the school are effective in promoting civic knowledge and engagement. In many countries, students who had participated in such experiences in school had greater civic knowledge and expectations to vote as adults compared to other students.
>
> (Kerr *et al.*, 2002: 5)

There are, however, some indications that pupil participation is beginning to be recognised as an important foundation for effective citizenship education. The Scottish Schools Ethos Network (described below) is an example of one innovative approach that places pupil involvement at the centre of its work.

The Scottish Schools Ethos Network (funded by the Scottish Executive Education Department and the University of Edinburgh) was established in 1995, as a network for schools interested in developing more positive learning cultures. The Network supports members in evaluating the ethos of their own setting through consultation with teachers, pupils and parents. Its key aims are to encourage schools to share ideas and approaches, to explore different ways of consulting and to develop new directions for improving their school ethos. The Network has encouraged schools to explore a number of key themes involving pupil participation and pupil consultation, including:

- overcoming barriers to pupil participation
- increasing pupil participation in school decision making
- developing the rights and responsibilities of children and young people
- promoting positive approaches to discipline
- including the potentially excluded.

Case studies describing some of the work carried out by Network member schools can be found at www.ethosnet.co.uk/casestudies.htm.

Conclusion

In this introduction, the outline of the case for involving pupils in improving teaching and learning has been presented as a pragmatic one but it must also be recognised that there are now ethical and legal dimensions. These dimensions stem, in part, from the United Nations Convention on the Rights of the Child (1989), an important international framework that has served as a catalyst for change in the way children and young people are viewed and treated in societies. The Declaration is premised on a set of ethical tenets asserting, for the first time, the rights of children as autonomous individuals. Its imperative for recognition of the child's right to have a voice in matters concerning his or her life adds further weight to the argument that young learners should be given opportunities to give their views on their education. However, as Morrow suggests, the influence of the Declaration has been more noticeable, in the UK, within legal and social work practice than education.

Indeed, the slow pace of progress was noted in the Euridem Project which reviewed pupils' involvement in decision making in education in four European countries (Denmark, Germany, the Netherlands and Sweden). The Project's researchers, Lynn Davies and Gordon Kirkpatrick, suggest that England and Wales are some way behind certain European countries in terms of a legal framework for pupil voice:

> England and Wales seem out of line with the rest of Europe in the way that young people have no legislated and government-supported ways to participate in decisions about their education. There are no ways in which they can be consulted regularly about educational policy.
>
> (Davies and Kirkpatrick, 2000)

In the chapters that follow, we will look at how schools are developing pupil consultation and pupil participation in different ways and explore the impact of these approaches on pupils, teachers and schools. Figure 1.2 summarises some potential benefits of pupil involvement at

For pupils,
involving pupils in discussion about teaching and learning:
- develops an understanding and awareness of learning processes
- helps pupils to see learning as a serious matter
- promotes the development of higher order thinking skills (meta-cognition)
- raises pupils' self-confidence and self-esteem
- allows pupils to acquire a 'technical language' for talking about learning.

For teachers,
involving pupils in discussion about teaching and learning:
- offers teachers feedback to help improve aspects of their practice
- can help to improve the quality of pupil–teacher relationships
- enables teachers to identify problems impeding pupils' progress
- helps to create a more collaborative classroom environment
- can be used to develop new ideas to improve teaching and learning.

For schools,
involving pupils in discussion about teaching and learning:
- may suggest new directions for school improvement planning
- can contribute to monitoring and evaluating processes for school self-review
- helps to establish a more positive learning culture within the school
- provides a practical expression of ideas taught in citizenship education
- encourages pupils and teachers to feel that they are valued and respected members of an inclusive, collaborative learning community.

Figure 1.2 Why pupil consultation is a key to improving teaching and learning – a summary

the three levels we have referred to in this introduction: individual pupil progress, classroom practice and whole-school development. It is also important to recognise the wider significance of pupil consultation and pupil participation in encouraging young people to see themselves as members of a learning community or, indeed, a learning society where learning is recognised and celebrated by all.

2 Consulting pupils: principles and approaches

Principles

The idea of talking about learning might seem to be an obvious and fundamental part of the teaching process but this kind of discussion is actually quite a rare feature of classroom life. As Britton suggests, talking about learning offers an opportunity for teachers to examine both sides of the teaching–learning coin, providing insights into how learning takes place and what factors can make a difference to pupils' achievement:

> If the teacher could be more certain what learning looked like, in some at least of its many guises, he [sic] might find it easier to 'monitor' his own teaching. Since learning doesn't take place to numbers, however, and will probably sometimes take place in a very disorderly fashion, it is impossible to set it out, marshalled and docketed like the exhibits in a museum. Glimpses of it are to be found, first, in what people say to each other.
>
> (Britton, 1969: 81–2)

Pupil consultation, however, takes the link between language and learning a step further than the descriptive analysis of classroom discourse that has been more commonly used in research on teaching and learning. Consultation offers a means by which young learners can be invited into a conversation about teaching and learning so that their role changes from being an 'object' of research attention to one of active participation. Moreover, as Nixon and colleagues

(1996) suggest, there is also evidence of the beneficial impact of such dialogue:

> Fostering dialogue at the classroom level, enabling the pupil's voice to be heard and valued, has the potential not only to improve relationships but to enhance the learning and achievement which policy makers seek.
>
> (Nixon *et al.*, 1996: 272)

Setting out to consult pupils about teaching and learning, however, presents new challenges as well as new opportunities and it must be acknowledged that the strategy carries some degree of risk for all concerned. Teachers may find that pupil consultation brings to light issues which are not simple and straightforward to address. The process itself can create or deepen tensions, either between staff members or between teachers and pupils. There may be reluctance among teachers and other members of staff to introduce change or to act upon pupil data; and there can be practical difficulties of finding the time and resources required. Pupils, too, may find consultation 'uncomfortable' because they may be worried that it could affect their relationships with peers; they might feel disappointed or frustrated when their views are sidelined and some may regard consultation with deep suspicion or a degree of anxiety because they are unaccustomed to having their views really listened to by adults.

Clearly, it is essential to plan very carefully before embarking on pupil consultation, taking into consideration factors such as the readiness of the school as well as practical issues of time management and resource availability. In this section, we look at the principles of pupil consultation and the different kinds of strategies that schools have used, giving attention to some of the key issues that need to be addressed in planning and developing consultation (see Table 2.1).

Approaches

Approaches to pupil consultation can be differentiated according to:

- *the extent of the initiative* (whether whole school, class or year group or identified groups of pupils)

Table 2.1 Preparing for consultation: some questions for schools to think about

• Readiness	Is this school ready to introduce pupil consultation strategies? Are teachers and pupils comfortable with the idea of consultation?
• Preparation	How should we set about consulting pupils? What kinds of issues should we look at? Do we need external support?
• Practical issues	Will the whole school or some year groups, departments or sub-groups of pupils be involved? What is the most appropriate timescale?
• Data gathering and analysis	How should data be gathered? Who will analyse the data?
• Using the findings	How can we use this information to improve teaching and learning? Is there a need for further information before new strategies are considered?
• Feeding back and communicating findings	How are the findings to be fed back to staff and pupils? Should the key findings be disseminated more widely?
• Monitoring and evaluating	What are the most effective ways of monitoring and evaluating strategies introduced through pupil consultation? Has the consultation process achieved its main objectives?

- *the scope* (focused on broad or narrowly defined concerns)
- *the timescale* (short, medium or long term)
- *the level of integration* of the initiative into the school's system and ethos (whether 'built-in' as an integral to the whole school, isolated in individual departments or limited to one teacher's interest and practice).

The broad approaches, described below, reflect these differences and some examples of each are presented to show how schools have

used these approaches and to outline some of the difficulties and benefits that have been encountered.

Pupil consultation approaches can be used:

- as a *'wide angle' approach* to identify generalised problems in schools
- as a way of focusing on *'spotlight' issues* of concern or on particular
  groups of pupils who are felt to need closer attention
- as part of school systems for *monitoring and evaluating* new strategies
  and interventions
- as a technique for *supporting individual learners* who are experiencing
  difficulties with their learning
- as part of the ongoing system for *school self-review*
- as a way of establishing a *more democratic school system* and putting
  citizenship education into action.

Which approach a school adopts will reflect its particular priorities for
action as well as its ethos and culture. As the profiles presented in this
section demonstrate, each school develops its own style of pupil consultation and approaches vary both in terms of the methods of consultation used and in the scale and scope of the initiative. In most cases,
the schools have been working with researchers from one of our projects
(see Appendix 3) and the teachers involved and the schools' senior
management teams have given permission for us to give an account of
their work. The profiles have been chosen to illustrate the different
approaches.

The 'wide-angle' approach

Pupil consultation is often used as a way of 'mapping the terrain' to
find out what is happening in a school or classroom. Teachers sometimes have quite general concerns that pupils are not performing as
well as they could and, in order to help them to understand why, they
have opened up a dialogue with pupils to explore their responses to,
and attitudes towards, particular aspects of teaching and learning. It is
also sometimes used within initiatives aimed at addressing broad issues
affecting a school's learning culture. It is particularly important in this
type of investigation that teachers do not set too much of the agenda
for discussion so that the exploration is a genuinely open one and that

hitherto unexamined issues can be brought to light. The following two profiles are of consultation in two comprehensive secondary schools but the approach has also been used successfully in a number of primary schools. Where the school was working with a project team, the project is identified in brackets and information about the individual projects can be found in Appendix 3.

Profile 1: Davison (Church of England) School for Girls (Improving Learning – The Pupils' Agenda)

About the school

Davison (CE) School for Girls is a single-sex comprehensive school for 12- to 16-year-olds in Worthing on the Sussex coast. Through a concerted effort by head teacher Sheila Wallis and her staff, pupil performance at the school has been raised significantly over the past few years, moving the percentage of pupils who achieve five or more A–C grades at GCSE from 30 per cent in 1988 to 71 per cent in 1998. The school has achieved one of the highest 'value-added' scores within West Sussex local education authority.

About the initiative

At Davison, the initiative for developing pupil consultation and pupil participation has been part of a long-term, whole-school endeavour and is very much a 'wide angle' approach. Dame Sheila Wallis has said that when she first arrived at the school over 15 years ago, the school's learning culture was seriously underdeveloped. She observed, for example, that there were markedly negative attitudes to learning among pupils and that many parents did not seem to take an active interest and involvement in their children's learning. There was also a sense of complacency among the teaching staff and Sheila felt that a 'culture of irrelevance' had become established across the whole school, with the result that many pupils thought that what went on in the classrooms bore little relationship to their futures.

Since her appointment as head, Sheila has tried to address these difficulties by introducing a series of strategies aimed at establishing a stronger sense of membership and community in the school. One example of the school's approach has been the *induction programme* presented to all new teachers and pupils, which provides them with a formal introduction to the school's philosophy, standards and expectations. *Pupil consultation* initiatives have also been integral to the overall strategy: pupils' views on various aspects of teaching and learning have been sought and acted upon. The school's concern to provide an *enriched curriculum* – with a vast array of lunchtime and after-school clubs and activities – has also reflected the school's objective to extend opportunities for more active participation by pupils in the life of the school.

Two fundamental principles underpinning the school's approach are that pupils must be treated in an adult way and that individuals have a right to be respected and accepted. These principles have helped to establish a more positive culture in the school and, when visited by members of the Improving Learning project research team, it was noticeable that pupils spoke with clarity and confidence about their learning. In interviews, pupils were happy to talk openly about their individual strengths and weaknesses in front of other pupils and there was no sense of embarrassment about achievement or about finding some aspects of learning more difficult. Indeed, many pupils at Davison seemed to recognise that everyone has weaknesses and strengths in one subject or another and that teachers and other pupils were there to support you through your difficulties.

The school has given whole-hearted commitment to demonstrating that, in all aspects of its life and work, *pupils matter*. This commitment has required giving attention to organisational aspects of schooling as well as what happens in the classroom. Four things stand out as characteristic of the Davison approach:

- a strong sense of membership and inclusiveness which is balanced by a clear appreciation of individual differences among pupils
- an emphasis on getting across to pupils the message that learning is 'for them' rather than something 'done to them'
- a clear respect for young people and a refusal to underestimate or ignore their capacities
- a firm commitment to providing both challenge and support for learning.

At Davison, demonstrating this principle that pupils matter has been more than simply a message about being a 'listening' school; it has reflected an overriding concern to support *all* pupils, whatever their interests and talents, to work at the limit of their capacity; it has been about ensuring that all pupils want to achieve and that the school does all it can to enable them to do so.

Comment

At Davison CE School for Girls, the development of pupil consultation and participation strategies has fed into a whole-school development programme based on the principle of showing pupils that they are valued and respected members of a learning community. The programme has contributed to the school's impressive achievements. It is important to recognise that this type of broad approach requires time and sustained effort to achieve its objectives – it is not a 'quick-fix' solution – and it needs the support and energy of a committed leadership team to ensure that the strategies introduced are sustained and become integrated into the school's systems and structure.

Profile 2: Falmer High School (ESRC/TLRP Project, Consulting Pupils about Teaching and Learning)

About the school

Falmer High School in Brighton (West Sussex local education authority) is a smaller than average comprehensive school, with around 700 pupils currently on roll, and serves a diverse community in this popular south coast resort. The local area is not a prosperous one and the school faces some challenges, as a recent OFSTED report inspection acknowledged:

> The percentages of students on the register of special educational needs (48 per cent), and with statements (4 per cent), are well above average. The local estate is a significantly deprived community, with many features of social and economic disadvantage which impinge on the school. The school population is not stable

as a significant number of students enter or leave between Years 7 and 11. Students enter the school with very low standards of attainment.

(OFSTED, 2001a: 7)

On taking up his appointment as head teacher, Antony Edkins recognised that addressing these challenges was a priority for the school and strategies were needed to develop a more positive learning culture. Pupil consultation and participation strategies were central to this improvement programme; teachers felt that these approaches would help to increase pupils' sense of membership of, and responsibility to, the school community. To further its pupil consultation strategy, the school accepted an invitation to participate in the ESRC/TLRP Project, Consulting Pupils about Teaching and Learning and worked on a project, led by John MacBeath and Kate Myers; the work undertaken by the school on this project is described below.

The project

Working with two tutor groups, one in Year 7 (11–12-year-olds) and one in Year 8 (12–13-year-olds), teachers used a variety of techniques to explore pupils' attitudes and responses to different styles of teaching and learning in the classroom and to gain a clearer picture of the factors that can affect pupils' engagement with learning. In a four-stage process that included pupils carrying out detailed observations of lessons and of individual pupils, data were gathered on pupils' responses to different learning tasks. These data were subsequently analysed to produce profiles of the target pupils' attitudes and responses. Key issues identified from the data were then used as a basis for focus group discussions with pupils.

Although the school had undertaken some pupil consultation previously, this project represented a completely new departure for teachers and pupils. The pupils who carried out the observations and took part in the subsequent discussion groups had not experienced such direct participation before, nor had they been involved in discussions with teachers focused on learning. In evaluating the project, teachers felt that both they and the pupils had benefited from the approach and a number of important issues were identified for follow-up. One issue raised was that pupils found active involvement in tasks enabled them to grasp difficult concepts more easily and carrying out these 'hands-on' activities often helped to increase their sense of motivation and engagement.

Pupils felt that taking part in this initiative had challenged their own preconceived ideas about particular aspects of teaching and learning. For example, some had gained a clearer understanding of the purpose of tests. Another interesting idea that emerged through these discussions was how pupils often took the lead from subtle signals from teachers about the nature of learning activities such as completing worksheets and homework assignments. If the teacher appeared more 'serious' about a particular task, then pupils tended to respond to this 'signal' by judging that the task must be important and so concentrated more thoroughly on it.

The school's unusual technique of using pupils to undertake observations, though limited in scale, provided a very useful platform for opening up issues in the focus group discussions. This approach was found to be manageable as it took only a short while for pupils to be trained in the observation techniques. The school, deeming it to be worth continuing, is now considering developing the approach, possibly with other year groups, to gain further insights into teaching and learning across the school.

Comment

The initiative described here demonstrates how an innovative strategy for consulting pupils can open up new areas of teaching and learning for discussion with pupils. The technique of pupils undertaking classroom observations was found to be an effective way of gathering data; it served as a way of increasing pupil involvement as well as encouraging teachers to share with pupils their perspectives on teaching and learning. It is important to note, however, that the school has a long-standing interest in pupil consultation and pupil participation and the initiative was an extension of this work. Where this kind of small-scale investigation is not part of a long-term development plan, however, there is a risk that changes introduced may be limited to those most directly involved in the project.

Spotlighting an issue

While the 'wide-angle' approach involves broad investigations of issues and concerns or reflects a school-wide commitment, the 'spotlighting issues' technique offers a more focused way to explore particular concerns in detail. Teachers who have used this approach have found it a helpful way of gaining insights into specific problems. Across schools a wide range of issues has been drawn under the spotlight including assessment, group work, science teaching, use of information technology and creative writing skills. Some schools have focused on certain pupil groups which are causing particular concern (for example, Year 3 (7–8-year-olds) and Year 8 have been looked at in some schools because of an observed dip in pupil performance).

Focusing on a specific issue or group, and using a clearly defined set of questions, has some advantages. It can be easier to translate findings into action and the more limited research frame allows teachers to work collaboratively with other colleagues or schools. It is important to acknowledge, however, that the approach does have some limitations. A particular drawback is that it is possible to miss out on important dimensions of pupil experience that have not been included within the restricted research parameters.

Profile 3: Little Stoke Primary School – focus on writing (ESRC/TLRP Project, Consulting Pupils about Teaching and Learning)

About the school

Little Stoke Primary School, Bristol, was opened in 1999 following the amalgamation of the local infant and junior schools. The school has around 350 pupils aged from 4 to 11 years currently on roll and serves a local community which includes a minority of diverse ethnic groups. Angela Greenwood, the head teacher, has been in post since the school's opening and the school has recently received an OFSTED commendation for improved levels of attainment. John Trimble is the school's deputy head teacher and he has a long-standing interest in encouraging pupils to think and talk about their learning. In 2000, the school applied to take part in 'Breaking New Ground' (part of the ESRC/ TLRP Project, Consulting Pupils about Teaching and Learning), to seek further support for John's research on developing collaborative ways of learning. The school was advised and supported in its research project by Eve Bearne, a research associate with the Faculty of Education (University of Cambridge) and Julia Flutter.

About the initiative

The school's initiative reflected three concerns. First, it was aware that some pupils did not seem to be achieving their potential with writing in the Key Stage 1 SATs: in particular, pupils who seemed capable of attaining Level 3 with writing were struggling to progress from Level 2. Second, it appeared that pupils were not enjoying creative writing tasks and teachers were concerned that they seemed to regard writing as simply a functional tool. A third issue was teachers' interest in developing collaborative working as a way of capitalising on pupils' ability to learn from each other. With these issues in mind, John Trimble decided to work with a selected group of pupils from his Year 2 class (6–7-year-olds) and developed paired and group work activities for use in teaching creative writing. He wanted to see whether working collaboratively in this way would help pupils to develop a clearer understanding of the quality of their writing – a necessary requirement for attaining Level 3 in writing – rather than concentrating only on the presentational and technical aspects of writing as they had done previously. John videotaped the target group's collaborative activity sessions and some extracts from these recordings were then shown to the whole class as a prompt for group discussions. This was an important facet of the research process, as John explains:

> The actual process of involving children in gathering and analysing data about how they are learning from each other is one in which the children are encouraged to talk about their own learning and continue to develop their understanding of the subject matter. For example, an analysis of the discourse between two children writing a story together and discussing which vocabulary to use might reveal that one child had a 'good idea' which the other had rejected. If these two children are asked to produce their analysis of the same discourse, from the child's perspective, this will help both to clarify the researcher's perspective and,

through discussion with the teacher/researcher, establish why this idea was rejected.

For John, an important dimension of pupil consultation and pupil participation also lay in the opportunity to gain a better understanding of children's 'cultural capital'. This refers to the experience and background that children bring into the classroom, shaping and colouring their engagement with learning in school. Through this project, as John explains, he has sought ways to move children forward with one aspect of their learning – creative writing:

> It is moving them beyond the culture that they come to school with that poses the problems and my hypothesis is that this will never take place through straightforward . . . plenary style, didactic teaching. A culture transfer is necessary which can only happen through discourse and exploration between children – with the children perceiving they have a vested interest in making this progress and, in writing at least, perhaps through an emphasis on narrative.

At the end of this one-year project, John reported that the target group of pupils had made progress in their creative writing skills and he noted particular improvements in the creative writing standards of some individual pupils. However, there were also some indications that the target group's attitudes to creative writing had become more positive and John noted that their enthusiasm had grown during the course of the year, evidenced by pupils bringing in stories they had written at home. Parents also commented that their children had begun to show an enjoyment of writing. John has decided to continue and extend his research to explore further ways of using collaborative techniques to support the development of pupils' creative writing skills:

> The whole aspect of what is, and how to encourage, effective group work is a continuing focus and next year I will spend more time involving the children in collaborating with me on trying to understand this, by watching and discussing clips of themselves, reviewing group work sessions, and also keeping group work diaries for making comments after a session.

Comment

Little Stoke Primary School's project has enabled John Trimble and his colleagues to gain a clearer understanding of how pupils think about collaborative group work and how this way of learning can be used effectively to help pupils improve the quality of their creative writing. The videotaped observation sessions appeared to be a useful tool for prompting discussion with pupils about the learning process while the recordings clearly helped to engage pupils' interest in the research.

Profile 4: Exmouth Community College – focus on science teaching (ESRC/TLRP Project, Consulting Pupils about Teaching and Learning)

About the school

Exmouth Community College is one of the largest comprehensive schools in the UK with around 2,400 pupils aged 11 to 19 years, over 400 pupils in each year group and a sixth form with around 300 pupils. Situated in the seaside town of Exmouth, in an area of outstanding natural beauty, some ten miles from the busy cathedral city of Exeter, the college is the only secondary school serving this diverse and widespread community with some pockets of social deprivation, described as 'amongst the most challenging in Devon'. There is also quite a high level of mobility in the local population and many pupils can experience some turbulence in their school careers as they move from school to school between Years 7 to 11.

In 2001, the college became involved in the ESRC/TLRP Phase 1 Project through its application to take part in the Breaking New Ground Project. Paul Freestone, then head of the school's science department, decided to explore pupils' views on teaching and learning in science and his work on this project was supported by Elaine Wilson, researcher and science lecturer (Faculty of Education, University of Cambridge) and Julia Flutter.

The college was aware that pupils at Key Stage 4 were underachieving in science compared with their performance in other GCSE subjects. Paul Freestone wanted to explore what lay behind these statistics by consulting pupils about their perceptions of science and science teaching. Consultation, he hoped, would offer the team of science teachers some new starting points to help raise pupil attainment.

About the investigation

Because of the large number of pupils in the year group it was decided that a sample group would be selected. A quarter of the Year 11 cohort was invited to participate in the investigation and the sample was balanced across the range of attainment (equal numbers were drawn from each ability group). The pupils responded confidentially to a questionnaire survey in which the following issues were addressed:

*   How interested are pupils in the sciences compared with other subjects?
*   How relevant do pupils perceive the sciences to be compared with other GCSE subjects?
*   How do pupils judge their own aptitude for learning science?
*   Are there differences between boys' and girls' attitudes to learning science?

The questions were based on research carried out by Pell and Jarvis (2001) who investigated primary aged pupils' attitudes to learning science. The data were analysed quantitatively and a summary of the findings was then fed back to the participating students and teachers in the science department. Key findings identified in the data included the following:

*   Only a few pupils ranked the sciences among their favourite subjects but pupils of all levels of attainment regarded the sciences as both important and relevant subjects.
*   Pupils were clear about the tasks, activities and teaching styles that they preferred in science but there were some striking differences in the choices expressed by pupils in higher and lower ability groups.
*   Although science was seen as an important subject, few pupils intended to take it in advanced courses or were considering a science-related career. The majority of those who were interested in studying science at a higher level were boys.

- Although enjoyment of the sciences was generally low, more pupils expressed a preference for biology than for physics or chemistry.
- There were clear differences in the preferences of boys and girls with regard to ways of working in science; the majority of girls liked to work collaboratively in science lessons while boys said they would rather work alone or in friendship pairs.

Pupils' responses to the question 'What aspects of science study do you enjoy?' highlighted differences between higher and lower attaining pupils. Higher attaining pupils expressed strong preferences for things like practical work and discussion in science lessons, whereas it was only the lower attaining pupils (both boys and girls) who mentioned the use of textbooks in science as being enjoyable. It was also noted that lower attaining pupils liked to carry out their own projects in science. It was these responses that prompted Paul to consider alternative teaching activities to encourage pupils' engagement with learning science.

After discussing his findings with both pupils and colleagues in the science department, Paul designed an intervention with groups of pupils across the attainment range to investigate their responses to an alternative way of learning science through individual project-based research on topics that interested them personally. The groups were invited to choose their own resources and source materials. Most began their projects by an Internet search of their chosen topic although subsequently most pupils turned to more traditional sources of information such as textbooks and library materials.

The evaluation of this intervention revealed that pupils had responded positively to this new way of working; they enjoyed working under their own initiative and had developed a strong sense of ownership of their work. Working independently in this way, with the teacher acting as a guide and source of support, appeared to boost their self-esteem and confidence in learning science. Tests at the end of the topic work showed an improvement in attainment for all ability groups involved in the project and these results were significantly higher than for the control groups who did not take part in the project. The findings have been disseminated to teachers in the science department who are now considering ways of developing the approach further to increase pupils' engagement with learning science.

Comment

This project set out with a clearly defined objective to improve teaching and learning in science, using pupil consultation to provide practical guidance for teachers in developing practice. Through the initial survey teachers were able to identify some interesting differences in pupils' responses to teaching and learning in science and these findings allowed them to pinpoint aspects of practice for further development. It is interesting to note that the differences in boys' and girls' responses to science have some parallels with the findings of other national research studies on this issue (see, for example, Parkinson *et al.*, 1998; Osborne and Collins, 2001).

In this initiative, Exmouth Community College used a large-scale survey technique to gather data. This approach yields a large volume of data and it is important to bear this in mind so that investigations are kept to a manageable size and timescale. In some cases, teachers have felt overwhelmed by large quantities of data and abandoned their research efforts because they could not find the time or resources to analyse this data. Monitoring and evaluating the approach are also essential to any intervention project because they help teachers to identify the benefits and disadvantages of the initiative and can be used in developing or refining the approach.

Monitoring and evaluating

This approach shares the narrow frame of the spotlight issues technique but has a more specific aim in that it uses pupil consultation to gather feedback on new strategies for improving teaching and learning. Quite similar in format to the familiar consumer survey, this approach is a useful way of sounding out pupil responses to new initiatives. It can also form part of long-term monitoring procedures (see also the section on 'In-school self-review', page 52). There are, however, some disadvantages and potential pitfalls that need to be borne in mind. One drawback lies in the quality of data obtained in these quick exercises. For example, using short, simple questionnaire surveys to gather data on pupils' responses may not give sufficient detail or accuracy because pupils might regard the questions as trivial and not take them seriously. Like the 'spotlight issues', this technique can also be somewhat limited in terms of impact and where it is used on a short-term or one-off basis it is unlikely to have a wider influence on teaching and learning within the school or on the school's ethos. If, however, it is built into a coherent, ongoing system for monitoring and evaluating school processes, and is given a high profile, then pupils and teachers will be more likely to recognise its value and it may then help to establish a more collaborative pupil–teacher relationship. The two profiles – one of a small primary school and one of a large, comprehensive secondary school – show how consultation can contribute to evaluations of new ways of working.

Profile 5: Harpfield Primary School – 'Making Choices': investigating the impact of choice on pupil learning (ESRC/TLRP Project, Consulting Pupils about Teaching and Learning)

About the school

Harpfield Primary School is a small primary school in Hartshill, Stoke-on-Trent. The school serves an area that has been quite seriously affected by social and economic hardship in recent years and this is evidenced in the higher than average number of pupils who are eligible for free school meals (currently around 21 per cent of the school roll). The school was one of six schools chosen to take part in Breaking New Ground (part of the ESRC/TLRP Phase 1 Project, Consulting Pupils about Teaching and Learning). Avril Vaughan, deputy head teacher, designed and carried out this project with advice and support from the Project research team (Julia Flutter and Nick Brown).

About the project

The school was concerned that a significant number of pupils appeared to be underperforming in all areas of the curriculum and it was felt that one of the main factors behind this underperformance was pupils' perceptions of the learning process. Although many pupils seemed motivated and wanted to do well, they sometimes did not understand what teachers expected of them and were unsure about how they could improve the quality of their work. Avril Vaughan believed that one way to help pupils to establish a stronger sense of ownership was by offering more choice in key areas of the curriculum. Avril carried out a one-year action research project with a selected group of pupils in her Year 5/6 class. The project had three interlinked objectives:

- to increase pupils' sense of ownership and autonomy by offering more choices
- to develop pupils' understanding of learning objectives and what they needed to do to achieve them
- to enable pupils to develop a vocabulary for thinking and talking about their progress in learning.

Twelve Year 5 pupils were selected to take part on the basis that they appeared to be performing below teacher expectations (these pupils were identified as being unlikely to achieve Level 4 in Year 6 SATs). At the outset some baseline data were gathered, using interviews and questionnaires, on pupils' attitudes and perceptions of learning and on their views of themselves as learners. Quantitative assessment data were also obtained, including test results from Year 4 (8–9-year-olds) and Year 5 optional SATs, spelling tests and teacher assessments. The intervention was carried out in the first two terms of the year and consisted of two teaching sessions per week, conducted by Avril. During the sessions the group was presented with exemplar materials that Avril had prepared to make the particular learning objectives of the session more explicit. Then pupils worked in small groups to discuss these learning objectives and were asked to suggest different ways of achieving them.

Avril reported that the pupils came up with an interesting variety of ways of meeting the learning objectives, including thinking skills techniques such as 'mind-mapping', collaborative ways of working, inviting guest speakers to tell them more about the topic, using information technology in various ways and accessing other special resources. As a result of these discussions lists of possible strategies were drawn up and the group then had to decide which idea to use to help them achieve the particular learning objective set for this unit of work. At the end of each session, pupils were asked to compare their work with original exemplar materials and to make an evaluation of their own efforts with support from Avril. At the end of the project pupils took part in a workshop organised with a local theatre group to explore the theme of 'choices' in learning.

Pupils' responses to the initiative were highly positive: they had clearly enjoyed taking part and had benefited from the experiences of making choices and decisions about their learning. There was also evidence of impact on their attainment: assessment of the target group's literacy, for example, showed measurable improvement and, interestingly, this improvement was greater than that achieved by pupils in a parallel Year 5/6 class. Avril's baseline data on the pupils' attitudes to learning in literacy, their initial views of themselves as writers and their understanding of learning objectives were compared with final evaluation data and the comparison showed pupils' increased understanding of learning objectives and a more sophisticated language for talking about their work and progress. The approach will be extended to other year groups and has been incorporated in the school's development plan.

Comment

This project demonstrates the benefits of promoting pupils' active participation in learning. Harris, reporting on a similar strategy, suggests that this way of working can have a positive impact on pupils' attainment:

> Effective teaching and learning was stimulated and strengthened when there was an attempt to involve pupils collaboratively in the learning process and where teachers encouraged pupils to work together . . .
>
> (1996: 65)

Avril has presented her findings to other members of staff and her experiences in working on this project have encouraged the school to continue developing the approach. Within the context of a small school, it is somewhat easier for innovative ideas to be communicated to the whole staff and for these ideas to take root. Such teacher-led, classroom-based investigations can provide important insights for teachers about how their pupils learn most effectively.

Profile 6: Rivington and Blackrod High School – developing effective target setting (ESRC/TLRP Project, Consulting Pupils about Teaching and Learning)

About the school

Rivington and Blackrod High School occupies two sites in Rivington, Lancashire – a pleasant, rural area not far from the industrial town of Bolton. The school was opened in 1973 following the integration of Horwich Technical School and Rivington and Blackrod Grammar School and currently has just over 1,900 pupils on its roll. In 2000 the school was designated as a Specialist Technology College. The school has Church of England voluntary controlled status and its Christian foundation is reflected in the school's ethos and traditions.

In 2000, the school submitted a proposal to the Breaking New Ground project (ESRC/TLRP Network Project) and was one of the six schools chosen to take part in the first round. Ingrid Cox, a senior teacher, coordinated the school's initiative and was supported by researchers Nick Brown and Julia Flutter.

About the initiative

The school was keen to monitor pupils' responses to recent developments in its target setting system for Key Stage 4 pupils. There were some concerns that this system might not provide the most effective way of supporting pupils in raising their standards of achievement. Ingrid Cox was keen to explore what kinds of support pupils actually found helpful at this stage in their school career and to see how they were coping with the pressures of these final two years.

To investigate these issues, Ingrid and her colleagues undertook a two-year project, examining pupils' views and perceptions over time and in some depth. Nine Year 10 pupils (14–15-year-olds) were selected to take part in the research, five boys and four girls, and this target group's range of attainment was broad. Teachers met with these students on a regular basis to discuss their progress and attainment and the mentoring process was then monitored by the research group during the two-year period.

At the outset of the project the pupils were also interviewed individually by researcher Nick Brown, to find out about their views of target setting and to gather baseline data on their attitudes to learning in Year 10 and on the school as a learning environment. Feedback from these initial interviews provided some valuable information on the school's target-setting practice and gave teachers a much clearer idea of the kind of support that pupils found helpful in improving their levels of attainment. The following extracts from the interview data illustrate the varied but constructive viewpoints expressed by these Year 10 pupils:

> It's [i.e. target setting] not been a very good process really. I've spoken to other people and they find it difficult if they're quite clever but their target grades are all A*s. They still find it difficult to achieve it and if they're not achieving it, well, they think, 'Well, why can't I be achieving it? This thing says I can but I'm not', so it puts pressure on a lot of people. Someone that knows you should sit down and speak to you and discuss where you are now and what you think you can achieve. So if you did it like that, then I think it would work. (Y10 pupil)

> [Target setting] encourages you . . . There's the target grade and you can try and beat it, try as hard as you can and try and beat it. (Y10 pupil)

> I don't think target setting's very useful because I don't think students themselves feel strongly about target grades. I don't personally know anyone who gets their target grades and thinks, 'Oh I'd better go home and do things better.' It's easier if the teacher has a word with you and says, 'Look, you're slipping in this' rather than having to set the grades. (Y10 pupil)

The interviews highlighted some specific drawbacks of target setting from the pupils' perspective. For example, some pupils found that being told that they would receive a poor grade affected their confidence; they seemed to think that the target setting grades delimited what they could achieve and so they tended to feel that there was little point in trying harder because they were unlikely to do any better, as this pupil explained:

> Because you know that's what you're targeted, you know that's what you've been set to get, you know that's all you can do. You

can tell your parents and they'll know that's all they can ask of you. (Y10 pupil)

Some pupils, however, were more positive about the target-setting process and felt it did encourage them to try harder and to pick up on areas of their work that required more effort. The opportunities to discuss their progress with teachers on an individual basis were particularly appreciated:

I was talking to my science teachers and they were saying that if I carry on the way I am doing then my target will be a C so [target setting] is working . . . (Y10 pupil)

To help teachers follow up the issues that emerged from the interview data, a one-day conference was organised in which teachers and pupils who had been involved in the project were invited to talk about the issues and to consider ways of developing the target-setting system and support arrangements for Year 10 and 11 pupils. The teachers and pupils who took part in this conference felt that it was a particularly valuable aspect of the project and pupils said that they would like to have further opportunities for such meetings. Ingrid Cox summed up the success of this conference in her final report:

Many of the pupil comments reflected a need to ensure that we have a school-wide approach to raising the debate about learning. This was an opportunity for students to give feedback about teaching and how this impacted on their learning. Lessons were learned, especially in the key subject areas. (Ingrid Cox, teacher, and research coordinator)

As a result of the initiative, the school has begun to develop a whole-school approach to target setting, giving a more active role to Year 10 and 11 pupils in deciding their targets and offering clearer guidance on ways of raising attainment in specific subject areas. One of the key findings gathered from pupil data was that pupils felt that they needed to know how to improve their work as well as what required improvement. The school is to continue monitoring its target-setting processes and is extending the school council brief to involve pupils in researching teaching and learning; and it is also developing a scheme for working collaboratively with local schools who are interested in developing pupil consultation strategies. Other key outcomes include an extension of the school's work on pupil participation through links with external organisations and a growth of interest among teachers in ways of developing pupils' vocabulary for thinking and talking about learning.

Comment

Although the main focus of the project was the school's development of a target-setting system, the investigation allowed other issues to be drawn into the research frame, and this helped teachers to gain a better understanding of the conditions of learning as Year 10 and 11 pupils experienced them. The project was unusual in having a longer timescale and this gave Ingrid and her colleagues an opportunity to track pupils' responses over time and to assess the impact of the mentoring on their final attainment.

The project's success was dependent on the sustained commitment of the research group of pupils and teachers. In her project report, Ingrid pointed out the advantages that she and her group found in being part of a wider project; it gave them access to support from experienced researchers who could offer advice and comment and enabled them to hear about the work that was going on in other schools, regionally and nationally. The school is keen to carry these developments forward in partnership with other schools and organisations.

Supporting individual learners

Consulting pupils about their learning on an individual basis and focusing on the need to talk about learning as a process are techniques which have been developed most widely in the field of special needs education where they have proved highly successful in improving pupil performance and in developing teaching practice (see Jelly *et al.*, 2000). In mainstream education, there has been increasing interest in mentoring schemes and similar types of individualised support. Although demanding in terms of time and resources, these developments have often proved valuable in supporting pupils' progress. A particular advantage in these one-to-one approaches lies in the opportunities they provide for pupils to engage in self-evaluation. As Black *et al.*

(2002) point out, these approaches have an important role in promoting independent learning:

> Pupils should be encouraged to keep in mind the aims of their work and to assess their own progress to meet these aims as they proceed. They will then be able to guide their own work, and so become independent learners.
>
> (Black *et al.*, 2002: 12)

Profile 7 describes one-to-one pupil consultation in action in a secondary school and is followed by an example of an innovative technique, developed by a practitioner in the special school sector, which provides a useful tool for accessing the views of pupils who find it hard to put their thoughts into words.

Profile 7: Kesteven and Grantham Girls' School (Improving Learning – The Pupils' Agenda)

About the school

Kesteven and Grantham Girls' School serves a largely rural area extending across three counties – Lincolnshire, Leicestershire and Nottinghamshire – but this widely dispersed school population includes only a few pupils who are eligible for free school meals and only three pupils who have statements of special educational need. Although the school has a very high level of achievement at GCSE the staff are committed to exploring ways of supporting all pupils in raising their achievement.

About the initiative

In 1998 the school took part in an initiative supported by Lincolnshire local education authority in collaboration with Jean Rudduck and Elaine Wilson from Homerton College, Cambridge, which focused on sustaining pupils' progress in learning during the early years of secondary schooling. The school decided to join this project because there was some evidence suggesting that pupils' engagement with learning appeared to slow down during Year 8. Losing ground at this early stage in secondary schooling may have a serious impact on individual pupil's progress and, according to national assessment data, this 'dip' in pupil performance may be quite a common phenomenon (Rudduck *et al.*, 1998).

Jane Batty, team leader for the school's science department, coordinated the school's research initiative in which one-to-one mentoring was introduced as a way of providing individualised support for Year 8 pupils. One-third of Year 8 pupils were mentored by volunteer pupils from Year 12 (16–17-year-olds), one-third were mentored by teachers and the remaining third were not offered a mentor. Training materials were prepared by Jane Batty and her team, and all Year 12 pupils and mentor teachers received this training prior to the mentoring sessions. The scheme was explained to the Year 8 pupils who were to receive the mentoring support and the Year 8 mentored pupils were randomly assigned to one of the three groups (mentored by Year 12 pupil; mentored by teacher; not mentored). Sessions were held once a fortnight during lunch breaks for up to twenty minutes in a large central space with informal seating.

The pilot scheme was carried out over one term and was subsequently evaluated through a questionnaire and interviews with pupils and mentors undertaken by linked researchers. Teachers were keen to monitor how pupils had responded to the mentoring.

A distinctive feature of the initiative lay in its capacity to offer general support on whatever issues pupils wanted to raise. Most concerns were about broad matters like managing time and priorities in relation to homework and revision, but some pupils wanted to talk about problems with particular subjects. For instance, some pupils who usually did well in a subject were worried about getting a bad mark for a particular piece of work and found it helpful to have someone to talk to privately about their feelings and concerns – or, as one pupil put it, 'to get it all off your chest'. One benefit of the school's initiative was that it helped to challenge the prevailing idea among pupils that it is unacceptable to acknowledge that you are struggling with your work. The pupils also identified several practical ways in which the mentoring sessions helped them: some said that they had learned how to manage their time more effectively or knew now where to find out the information that they needed. Sometimes mentors had provided encouragement for pupils to speak to a particular teacher about the specific difficulties that they were experiencing in their subject. It was also possible for pupils who were privately pleased about something they had achieved, in or out of school, to share their success with someone else without embarrassment: 'It meant I could tell someone about the good things that were happening'.

Evaluation of the mentoring scheme provided helpful information on successful aspects of the scheme as well as pinpointing difficulties and areas that might need further development. As part of the evaluation, the mentored pupils were interviewed again by one of the link researchers and invited to give their views on the mentoring process. In these interviews, Year 8 pupils were clear about the qualities that made a 'good mentor'. They said that the mentor needed to be someone who:

- can be relied upon
- is approachable, a good listener and is interested in what you have to say
- has the skill to encourage you to talk and is not intrusive or pushy
- is knowledgeable and experienced.

One pupil summed up these qualities when she explained that a good mentor is:

> . . . someone who seems interested in what you're saying even if to them it's not interesting. Your problems might seem really minor to them because they're older and probably they've experienced bigger problems than yours but they have to act as though they're interested in what you're saying.

All the pupils interviewed by the researcher thought that the scheme should continue and some suggested sensible modifications such as holding longer sessions or using a quieter, more 'private' venue. Overall, the evaluation evidence suggested that the initial pilot scheme was successful in supporting pupils to address some of the difficulties they experienced in Year 8 and pupils appreciated the opportunity to talk about their learning. The initiative demonstrated pupils' capacity to comment constructively and intelligently, when invited to do so, on things in school that make a difference to their learning.

Comment

Mentoring schemes such as this one are becoming an increasingly common feature in secondary schools, though they are more usually offered to pupils in Key Stage 4 who are felt by teachers to be at risk of underachievement. The school's use of pupils as mentors is more unusual although peer support is quite widely used in anti-bullying strategies. James *et al.* (1992) developed a similar peer mentoring strategy in which older secondary pupils acted as mentors for younger secondary pupils who were experiencing difficulties with their learning. The researchers reported that the approach had beneficial outcomes for both the older and younger pupils involved: in particular, it was noted that the older pupils felt that their confidence and sense of empathy had increased.

A valuable aspect of Kesteven and Grantham's approach was its use of pupil commentary as an evaluation tool. The interviews gave pupils an opportunity to comment on the mentoring process itself, enabling teachers to assess whether the strategy was providing effective support and to identify ways of improving it. Like teachers at Rivington and Blackrod High School, Jane Batty and her colleagues at Kesteven and Grantham Girls' School felt that they had benefited from participation in a wider project because they had been able to discuss their ideas and experiences with teachers in other schools and they could draw on the expertise of outside researchers.

Profile 8: Working with 'Angela' – Patricia Galbraith, counsellor (Network member of the ESRC/TLRP Project, Consulting Pupils about Teaching and Learning)

Patricia Galbraith is a professional counsellor and teaching assistant who works in a school for children with special educational needs in the north-east of England. This profile is based on Patricia's account of her work with 'Angela'. (For reasons of confidentiality, this is not the pupil's real name and the school has not been identified). This profile presents an unusual technique for supporting individual pupils whose difficulties with learning reflect some complex considerations. Patricia's approach encourages both visual and verbal means of expression to enable pupils like Angela, who do not find it easy to express their ideas, to participate more fully in the consultation process.

The approach

Angela is a 15-year-old pupil who attends the special school where Patricia Galbraith works. Angela has suffered mild cerebral palsy and her difficulties with learning are exacerbated by her poorly developed social skills and behavioural problems. Angela's academic progress is patchy and she has had particular difficulty with acquiring literacy skills. In this extract from her account of her work with Angela, Patricia describes Angela's typical pattern of behaviour in classroom situations:

> When Angela enters the classroom at the start of the school day, she inevitably finds a desk where she can sit on her own. Moreover, she does not speak unless she is spoken to and even then she does not always answer. When she does reply to a greeting or a question, it tends to be a mumble and often she covers her mouth whilst she is speaking. Because of these poor social skills, it is extremely difficult for Angela to relate to either peers or adults, which contributes to a poor self-image and low self-esteem.

Although Angela seemed to perform well in some subject areas, any aspect of the curriculum requiring social participation (for example, group discussion or reading aloud) was clearly problematic and in these situations her behaviour was characterised either by a quiet withdrawal or by inappropriate, and sometimes aggressive, responses.

Patricia's research aimed to help Angela to improve her behaviour and performance by developing better social and communication skills through one-to-one discussions; the discussions would explore the difficulties she was experiencing with her learning at school. Angela's parents, and other teachers at the school, also worked closely with Patricia to identify the various factors that seemed to affect Angela's behaviour. It became apparent that it deteriorated at quite specific points during the school day (notably during 'unstructured' periods such as break time) and in certain areas of the school. Having identified these 'problem' patches, the next step was to talk to Angela to find out why she was responding in this way and to help her to find strategies to enable her to cope with these situations.

Patricia's one-to-one sessions with Angela took place in a comfortable setting where Angela could feel secure. Nevertheless, Angela's reactions to these sessions were initially mixed, as Patricia explains:

> Working with Angela proved to be easier than I had anticipated, as she seemed to be more responsive in a one-to-one situation ... [however] there were occasions when she refused to answer me, or even to look at me. I responded to her reluctance to communicate with firmness, detachment and patience. However, I continued to show uncompromising acceptance of her as a person.

The sessions with Angela, and information from teachers and her parents, suggested that one of the factors behind her low self-esteem was that she did not feel that she had any degree of responsibility conferred on her, either at home or at school. To find out more about Angela's perspectives on her world, Patricia gave her a digital camera and invited her to take photographs around the school of places that she liked. At first, Angela was nervous about doing this but her confidence soon increased and she began to enjoy the task. Discussing the photographs with Patricia was valuable: it helped to highlight areas of the school where Angela felt at ease and enabled Angela to talk about her feelings in places where she felt unhappy or insecure. A further benefit of the photographic approach was that being given responsibility to manage a piece of equipment appeared to boost Angela's confidence.

After six months of working in this way with Angela, Patricia feels that her approach has achieved some positive outcomes, although some aspects of Angela's difficulties remain unresolved. Patricia reports that the sessions have led to an improvement in Angela's understanding of social relationships and that this has helped her to deal with classroom situations that she had previously found problematic.

Patricia summarised the reasons why the approach was successful for Angela:

- The individualised attention Angela received through the project helped her to feel 'special' and clearly had a positive impact on her attitudes and self-perception.
- Having to accept responsibility and being trusted to look after the camera helped Angela to feel that she was trusted and this increased her self-confidence.
- The opportunity to make choices (selecting what she would take photographs of) was a new experience for Angela and, although challenging for her at first, became easier as her confidence increased.
- Working with Patricia helped Angela to develop a better understanding of social situations and she has now begun to make friends.

The strategy Patricia has developed in her work with Angela offers useful guidance on ways of working with individual pupils who are experiencing difficulties with their learning and may be adapted according to the particular needs of the pupils concerned.

Comment

There are many examples of mentoring in schools and individualised approaches, such as this one, demonstrate the potential of one-to-one consultation for making a real difference to pupils' chances of success in school. The study also presents an innovative technique of gathering data using a visual approach (through Angela's digital photography); it offers a way of accessing pupils' perceptions of their learning environment that does not depend wholly on verbal skills.

One-to-one strategies such as this are, of course, heavily time-consuming. Schools may need additional support and advice in cases where pupils have complex emotional and behavioural problems. However, as this example demonstrates, the strategies may be worth the extra time and effort required because, for pupils like Angela, they can be a way of restoring their chances of successful learning.

In-school self-review

Interest in school self-review is growing in the wake of much publicised concerns with government inspection systems. There are clear benefits for schools in establishing effective mechanisms for reviewing their own performance (for further discussion, see MacBeath and McGlynn, 2003). Pupil consultation has a key role to play in these systems, both in social and academic terms. Pupils' perspectives can provide useful information about the quality of teaching and learning and the consultation process itself can help to establish a stronger sense of community. The following profiles show how two schools developed self-review approaches incorporating pupil consultation techniques.

Profile 9: The Sweyne Park School – pupil consultation as part of in-school self-review

About the school

The Sweyne Park School is an 11–16 comprehensive school situated on the outskirts of Rayleigh in Essex and was opened in 1997 following the amalgamation of two former secondary schools. Although the school itself is non-selective, the local area is one in which selection takes place and the attainment of pupils on intake in Year 7 is described as below the national average. In recent years, the school has seen a significant rise in its GCSE performance and, in the school's latest OFSTED inspection report, its teaching and learning was described 'very effective'. The school has an active interest in teacher research and has taken part in several research initiatives including the ESRC/TLRP Project, Consulting Pupils about Teaching and Learning. The work described in this profile, however, is part of its ongoing programme of in-school self-review.

About the initiative

Head teacher Kate Spiller has a firm commitment to involving pupils in the school's development and planning, and pupil consultation is regularly undertaken, forming a key element in monitoring and evaluating teaching and learning across the school. In recent departmental reviews pupils were consulted through questionnaires on their views of teaching in different subject areas and the data have enabled teachers to identify where improvements to practice can be made. The school has also involved pupils, through consultation and discussion, in developing its OFSTED Action Plans.

An example of a pupil questionnaire is shown in Table 2.2 (this format was compiled by teachers and is adapted for use in various departments). These simple, straightforward surveys are analysed quantitatively to give teachers a snapshot of pupils' responses to aspects of teaching and learning in each subject area; supplementary interviews and observations are carried out to give a more complete picture of pupils' responses.

Comment

Unlike many projects and initiatives described in this chapter, Sweyne Park's work has not been part of an external research project, although the school does maintain links with other schools interested in pupil consultation through the ESRC/TLRP Network and it was formerly involved in the Homerton–Schools Research Circle. The school has developed its own systems for consulting pupils as part of its school self-review programme and the senior management team has given a high priority to this reviewing process which allows teachers, pupils and parents to feel that their views are listened to and, wherever possible, will be acted upon. The effectiveness of this approach is difficult to quantify but it has clearly contributed to the positive developments identified by OFSTED: 'These high standards result from the good teaching which pupils experience and their own very good attitudes to school and to learning' (OFSTED, 2001b).

However, this approach demands a fairly large investment of teacher time. Teachers have felt that this investment has been worthwhile because it has helped to establish a positive learning culture across the school. A caution, however: surveys *can* be carried out too often, leading pupils to become bored with constantly filling in questionnaires and, consequently, giving answers that are not fully considered or serious. This seems not to have happened at Sweyne Park – because pupils believe that they are making a worthwhile contribution to improving teaching and learning in the school.

Table 2.2 The Sweyne Park School: pupil questionnaire

GENDER_____   YEAR GROUP_____

For each of the following questions circle one of the four answers.
Please answer honestly.

Does your teacher:

1	Explain things clearly?	Always	Often	Sometimes	Never
2	Say 'well done' when you do some good work or try very hard?	Always	Often	Sometimes	Never
3	Seem enthusiastic about the subject?	Always	Often	Sometimes	Never
4	Show they know the subject well?	Always	Often	Sometimes	Never
5	Encourage everybody to take part in the lesson?	Always	Often	Sometimes	Never
6	Expect high standards of work from you?	Always	Often	Sometimes	Never
7	Explain what the rules are when working in the class?	Always	Often	Sometimes	Never
8	Expect high standards of behaviour from you?	Always	Often	Sometimes	Never
9	Quickly go over the work you have just done when starting a new lesson, if appropriate?	Always	Often	Sometimes	Never
10	Make it clear what you are expected to do and learn each lesson?	Always	Often	Sometimes	Never
11	Summarise what you should have learnt at the end of the lesson?	Always	Often	Sometimes	Never
12	Set the right amount of homework?	Always	Often	Sometimes	Never
13	Set work which is too hard?	Always	Often	Sometimes	Never
14	Set work which is too easy?	Always	Often	Sometimes	Never

Profile 10: Langdon School – pupil involvement in school review and planning (ESRC/TLRP Project, Consulting Pupils about Teaching and Learning)

About the school

Langdon School is one of the largest comprehensive schools in the UK and serves an inner city community in north-east London (in the Borough of Newham). The school has pupils from a wide range of ethnic groups, many of whom have only recently arrived in the UK, including some refugees from war-torn countries. Over 50 per cent of pupils are eligible for free school meals and the majority of pupils speak English as an additional language. Due to its active, innovative programme for school development and improvement, the school has been involved in the Beacon Schools programme. Particular strategies that the school have focused on: leadership and management; school self-evaluation; raising pupil expectations and achievement; the inclusion of pupils with special educational needs; student involvement in school planning and a study support programme.

About the initiative

On her appointment as head, Vanessa Wiseman was concerned that the school's performance data indicated that many pupils were not achieving their full potential and this was a priority for the school's development plan. A crucial starting point, she believed, was to generate a more positive climate for learning in which pupils felt that it was not only possible but also legitimate for them to work hard and to achieve to the best of their abilities. Rather than focusing on specific issues or pupils, Vanessa and her team decided that the school had to try 'redrawing the big picture' through a whole-school development programme aimed at raising standards of attainment. The key objectives were to introduce strategies that would serve to emphasise and promote pupils' success and achievement; to give pupils opportunities for more active involvement in the life of the school; and to help pupils feel a sense of ownership of, and responsibility for, their learning and success. Creating a positive learning culture became a guiding principle woven into all aspects of the school's work and the programme's strategies operated at two distinct levels. At one level, strategies were introduced to develop pupils' confidence and self-esteem through offering opportunities to take responsibility and to have a voice in the life of the school. At another level, strategies have been directed at improving aspects of teaching and learning across the school. These learning-focused schemes have included tailored support for pupils experiencing difficulties with particular aspects of their learning, a peer mentoring system and after-school provision, such as the home-work club and study centre which offer vital facilities for pupils who lack suitable workspace and resources at home.

As a result of the school's interest in consulting pupils as part of school self-review, it was invited to take part in the ESRC/TLRP Project, 'Consulting Pupils about Teaching and Learning', in an initiative with other schools, led by John MacBeath and Kate Myers (for further details see Appendix 3). Through its involvement in this project, Langdon School decided to explore ways of extending its use of pupil consultation within school self-review and these were some of the strategies introduced through the project:

- pupil consultation about the school's system of target setting
- pupil participation in lesson evaluations
- pupil involvement in developing the school's Teaching and Learning Policy and pupil consultation on matters relating to the school's OFSTED Action Plan
- facilitation of an ongoing dialogue between teachers and pupils about learning.

The school had also been involved in an earlier research project, 'Improving Learning – The Pupils' Agenda', which looked at how schools were developing pupil consultation approaches to improve teaching and learning. The project researchers found the school's approach using regular consultation with pupils had not only provided a useful channel of communication and source of ideas for develop-ment strategies but also helped to create a 'community' atmosphere in the school and pupils seemed to respond well to its inclusive, respectful ethos. One Year 8 pupil summed up his view on the sense of participa-tion that many pupils appeared to share: 'It's not just for the adults to do everything – the children get involved too.'

Comment

Langdon's programme of pupil consultation and pupil participation has become an established part of the school's learning culture. The success of the programme has been widely recognised, as is evidenced by the large numbers of visitors to the school who come to witness the school's achievements for themselves. Sustaining the momentum of this type of approach is not always easy but Langdon has been able to do so largely because the school's senior management team is firmly committed to the principles of pupil consultation and participation and has ensured that these ideas are integrated into all aspects of the school's work. Again, there has been a concerted attempt to involve the school in external networks – including the European SOCRATES initiative, a local community forum and with Beacon partner schools – so that teachers can draw on guidance and ideas from other schools, higher education and national agencies.

Teaching about citizenship

The recently introduced curriculum guidance on citizenship education requires that schools teach pupils about the nature and purpose of democracy and introduce them to the idea of the rights and responsibilities of membership of a democratic society. For pupils in Key Stage 3 and 4 this is a statutory component of the National Curriculum.

Pupil participation and pupil consultation are acknowledged as social vehicles through which the aims of citizenship education can be advanced – if enacted in the daily life of the school. As Qualifications and Curriculum Authority (QCA) guidelines for schools point out, involving pupils in this way represents rather more than a 'bolt-on' extra to more traditional styles of teaching citizenship education:

> Opportunities for pupils to become helpfully involved in the life of the school are essential forms of learning in citizenship and can provide coverage of the requirements in the programmes of study.
>
> (QCA, 2000: 12)

Others have taken this argument further, proposing that participation and active involvement by young people in school matters are, in fact, the only effective ways of teaching about citizenship and democracy. Roger Hart argues that 'Only through direct participation can children develop a genuine appreciation of democracy and a sense of their own competence and responsibility to participate' (1997: 3). However, as Ryan points out, there is a need to ensure that such participation represents a genuine, rather than token, opportunity for pupils:

> From what students say of their schools as political environment, one must conclude that if students are to learn in school the habits of adult responsibility, only the habit and expectation of participation in decisions of actual moment to the participant can be effective education for adult citizenship.
>
> (1976: 9)

The most common approach for introducing pupils to the ideas of democracy in the UK has been the school council. Over the past decade, there has been an increase in the number of school councils in both the primary and secondary sectors, and there are signs that the traditional brief of these councils – to discuss practical issues (such as lockers, uniforms and facilities) and social aspects of school life (including fundraising and special events) – is now widening to embrace matters relating to teaching and learning. Tany's Dell Primary School (see below), like many other primary schools, has a pupil council for pupils but its commitment to a democratic approach takes it a step further as it seeks to establish a learning community which everyone feels a part of.

Profile 11: Tany's Dell Primary School – creating a positive learning culture (Improving Learning – The Pupils' Agenda, a project supported by the Nuffield Foundation)

About the school

Tany's Dell Primary School is in Harlow, one of Essex's 'new towns', and the local community includes many families who have moved in from other areas. The town has had quite a high level of unemployment and some families are socially disadvantaged. The school's most recent OFSTED report (1997) noted that many pupils entered the school with poor language skills, and behavioural problems were also common. In spite of these challenges, the school has created a positive learning environment in which pupils, parents and teachers share a sense of common endeavour. As part of this approach, the school has tried to improve communications between teachers, pupils and parents and its efforts to improve home–school liaison were recently praised in an OFSTED inspection (OFSTED, 1997). Another dimension of its positive ethos is the school's interest in creating a democratic school community, based on pupil consultation and pupil participation strategies. In 1998, the school's innovative work led to an invitation to take part in a national research study, Improving Learning: The Pupils' Agenda (supported by the Nuffield Foundation), coordinated by Jean Rudduck and Christine Doddington.

About the initiative

Teachers at Tany's Dell had been concerned that many pupils seemed to lack confidence and appeared to have low levels of self-esteem; teachers felt that these problems were having a negative impact both on pupils' performance in school and their relationships with teachers and other pupils. The difficulties arising from these personal problems were clearly apparent in the high incidence of behavioural difficulties noticed during lunch and break times. To address these issues, the school decided to look for ways of helping pupils to develop more positive self-images and to see themselves as valued members of a learning community. As a first step, the school tackled the immediate problem of pupils' unacceptable behaviour in the playground and classrooms by introducing a positive behaviour programme. This programme proved highly successful in reducing the incidence of problem behaviour and teachers noticed a calmer, happier atmosphere developing within the school. Following the introduction of the behaviour management programme, which gave pupils a stronger sense of security, further strategies were introduced to raise pupils' self-esteem:

- Every pupil became a 'special' person in their class for one week during which their achievements were celebrated by the class ('person of the week' scheme).

- Pupils were given opportunities to take responsibility for aspects of the school environment and suggest how they would like to improve the school.
- The school council (known as the Children's Committee) became directly involved in school development planning – thus demonstrating that their views were respected and valued.
- Improved Communication with parents was improved through a system of home–school books detailing pupils' progress and achievements and special 'open afternoons' were held where parents could see pupils' work.
- Special displays were set up in prominent places to showcase pupils' best work.
- Whole-school assemblies were held to celebrate pupils' achievements.

Linking these strategies was the school's principal concern – to encourage pupils to take responsibility both for themselves and for others and to recognise their rights and responsibilities as members of a learning community. Some elements of the approach are often found in primary schools but, at Tany's Dell, these elements have been drawn together into a coherent policy that is fully integrated into the school's ethos and practice. There is clear evidence that pupils are responding to this distinctive ethos and, in interviews with the Improving Learning project's link researcher, pupils spoke with pride and warmth about what they called the 'the Tany's Dell way of doing things'.

At Tany's Dell, the ethos is a firmly democratic one; the principle that everyone has a contribution to make to the life of the school underpins all areas of its work. The key values that the school tries to convey are these:

- *Everyone* is entitled to work in a caring, happy and safe environment.
- *Everyone* should feel that they are learning something new and meaningful.
- *Everyone* is valued.
- *Everything* done in school has a purpose and a reason.
- *Everyone* in school aims to be open, honest and truthful.
- *Everyone* in the school should feel that they trust each other.

A notable feature of pupil interview data was the strong expression of care and responsibility among pupils of all ages. It was evident that older pupils felt that they could be open with teachers and with each other and they saw themselves as being part of a 'learning partnership'. Pupils' comments also revealed how much they valued teachers' efforts to make work exciting and challenging and they liked the fact that, if certain 'mundane' tasks had to be done, teachers took time to explain why these were important for their learning. As one pupil explained: 'If it's boring [work] teachers apologise to you.' Interestingly, in one group interview, pupils said that making lessons 'fun' was not only important for pupils but it was also important that teachers should also enjoy what they were doing. For further details on the school's approach see the Project report (Doddington *et al.*, 1999).

Head teacher Val Jones stressed that the whole school learning environment is built on emphasising the positive and she believes that this has been a key to its success. This ethos has been particularly important given the experiences of the local community, where unemployment and other social problems have left some families facing hardship and feeling 'devalued'. The school's focus on positive feedback and promoting active involvement has extended well beyond the school gates and has helped to engage the local community in the day-to-day life of the school.

Comment

Rather than implementing discrete strategies, the school has worked on a multifaceted programme centred on its commitment to a democratic ethos. Although behaviour management, for example, was identified as an immediate priority, rather than concentrate their efforts wholly on tackling behaviour difficulties as they arose, teachers looked at the reasons for unacceptable behaviour and addressed the wider problems emanating from pupils' low self-esteem. It was also apparent that involving pupils in developing strategies for dealing with problem behaviour in the playground was effective. Other research studies have confirmed that giving pupils some degree of ownership and responsibility in resolving these problems is important (Sharp *et al.*, 1994).

Profile 12: Sandringham School – developing the role of the school council (ESRC/TLRP Project, Consulting Pupils about Teaching and Learning)

About the school

Sandringham School in St Albans, Hertfordshire, was opened in 1988 following the amalgamation of two secondary schools in the area. The school is a popular comprehensive school with a sixth form. It has gained a high reputation in the local community and is heavily over-subscribed. The school's most recent OFSTED report gave particular praise to the school's positive ethos:

> The school's mission is to enable 'everybody to be somebody' through recognising and developing students' individual abilities and personal motivation; developing students' confidence and belief in themselves as successful young people; providing an exciting environment in which students will develop a love of learning; setting and celebrating the achievement of high personal goals.
>
> (OFSTED, 1999)

About the initiative

The school had an established ethos affirming the value of dialogue between pupils and teachers, and head teacher Janet Lewis was keen to look for ways of extending this approach further. A range of strategies involving pupil consultation and pupil participation were introduced in response to the school's guiding principle of enabling 'everybody to be somebody'. The success of this approach was apparent in pupils' strongly positive attitudes towards learning and to the school. Teachers believed that one of the most significant benefits of the school's approach lay in its impact on the quality of pupil–teacher relationships.

Although the school had given pupils opportunities to be involved in decision making and regularly sought pupils' opinions (for example, pupils were invited to interview applicants for teaching positions), Janet Lewis and her staff were keen to try out different ideas for consulting pupils about aspects of teaching and learning. The school decided to participate in the ESRC/TLRP Project, Consulting Pupils about Teaching and Learning, to support further development of these approaches. Working with a group of primary and secondary schools around the country, the school explored some new ideas for pupil consultation, including the use of pupil evaluations in reviewing assessment practices and setting up focus groups with pupils in Years 8, 9 (13–14-year-olds) and 10 to examine ways of improving the school's system of Records of Achievement.

Teachers at Sandringham School are convinced of the importance of establishing an ongoing dialogue with pupils, but in interviews with the ESRC/TLRP Project team, some said that it is important that schools give careful consideration before introducing this type of approach; schools need to be sure that they are 'ready' to engage with pupils in a partnership. They felt that the approach only works: '. . . when you have effective relationships'; 'when there's mutual respect between staff and pupils'.

Sandringham School has involved the school council in a wide range of decision-making processes and has established a system for pupil consultation that allows teachers to listen and respond to pupils' perspectives on teaching and learning. The school's belief is that giving pupils opportunities to take a more active role in the life of the school, and by taking their views seriously, pupils feel valued and important and this, in turn, enhances their commitment to learning and achievement.

Comment

Although school councils are increasingly common and provide a useful means of introducing the key principles of citizenship and democratic systems, they are rarely concerned with issues directly relating to teaching and learning. A further disadvantage in the school council approach is that, in many cases, it is only a minority of pupils who have a direct involvement in the council's activities.

Both Tany's Dell and Sandringham schools have looked beyond the school council in seeking ways to encourage pupils to feel a sense of membership of, and responsibility towards, their school community. The Sandringham School approach includes some unusual approaches for developing pupils' active participation in the life of the school, such as pupils' involvement in staff recruitment interviews. These approaches have raised the profile of the school's strategies for pupil consultation and participation so that they are not limited to a small number of pupils but have a direct influence on the school as a whole. The impact of this approach is clearly demonstrated in comments made during the school's most recent OFSTED inspection (1999) in which inspectors noted the mutual high regard that characterised pupil–teacher relationships across the school.

Profile 13: Hastingsbury Upper School and Community College – the growth of the Student as Researcher Group (ESRC/TLRP Project, Consulting Pupils about Teaching and Learning)

About the school

Hastingsbury Upper School and Community College is in Kempston, Bedfordshire. The school, which opened in 1970, has pupils aged between 13 and 19 years and it enjoys close links with the local community, with around 2,000 people attending its part-time education courses. It is non-selective and the majority of its pupils have previously attended one of the two local middle schools; most pupils remain in the school for post-16 studies. In 1999, the school was one of six selected to participate in Breaking New Ground (part of the ESRC/ TLRP Project, Consulting Pupils about Teaching and Learning). Teacher-researcher Gill Mullis has coordinated the school's research initiative with support from the Project team.

About the initiative

At the outset of the project, Hastingsbury Upper School had already established its structure for a student council; it adopted a rather unusual system for pupil representation, with each year cohort having its own, fully autonomous council comprised of representatives from each tutor group. There is no whole-school council. Each year council is formally structured with pupils taking on responsibility for roles of Secretary, Chair, Vice-Chair and Treasurer and the councils are allocated a small budget. The council members have also received some training and older councillors are expected to cascade these skills by training younger councillors.

Gill Mullis coordinates and supports these year councils and her project aimed to extend their brief beyond the traditional concerns by encouraging them to focus on pupil involvement in decision making within the school and on matters relating to teaching and learning. Working with the year councils, Gill suggested that they could set up a sub-committee to research aspects of teaching and learning that pupils felt were important. The pupils who volunteered to join the research group were given some guidance on research techniques to help them carry out their investigations. The training was seen as helpful:

> We wouldn't be this far without the training. We've developed knowledge about research methods and got a sense of direction. (Y11 student councillor)

The first issue raised was 'What makes a good lesson?' and the pupil researchers decided to explore the factors and conditions that combine to make a successful learning experience. The staff have been kept fully informed of the group's activities. The research group has already produced a skeleton 'model' of what makes a good lesson, based on initial discussions with pupils, and this is to be followed up through a survey, interviews with staff and pupils and classroom observations.

One of the most interesting aspects of this initiative has been its impact on communication between teachers and pupils. The presentations, both within the school and at conferences, have been well received by teachers in the school, in the feeder middle schools and at conferences. These are some comments made by the Year 11 councillors:

> I'm more confident. My English has improved. I type up everything and distribute it and giving presentations, my oral work, things like that, don't bother me any more. Thirty teachers, six different schools, it doesn't bother me now to stand in front of the class, or, the other day, to speak to our old Middle School teachers. (Y11 pupil councillor)

> We've got a staff meeting next week and there are students who want to say something so they're coming along. Now it's just accepted that there will be meetings where they come along and

share their research and then they speak for themselves and there are very few staff who aren't actually interested in what they're saying. (Gill Mullis, teacher-researcher)

Although the initiative is still developing there are indications that it is prompting some change in the relationships within the school and that a process of dialogue about teaching and learning has been initiated. Gill Mullis recently gave this description of the initiative's progress:

We began with the aim of developing students' involvement in decision making within the school by working with Student Council members. In doing so, we slowly defined the 'we', began to challenge discourse and practice which excluded students from decision making, and transformed the 'that' – no longer a discussion about paint pots and social areas, but a dialogue about relationships and teaching and learning. (Gill Mullis, teacher-researcher)

Comment

Hastingsbury Upper School found that being part of wider networks (including the Bedfordshire Schools Improvement Project and the ESRC/TLRP Network Project) provided valuable sources of support and has offered opportunities for pupils and teachers to exchange ideas with other schools. However, a particularly important dimension of this initiative was the training that pupils received, both in developing their roles as councillors and in learning about research methods. As Charlton points out, the need for training pupils is an important consideration in developing effective strategies for pupil participation:

Teachers have remarked that pupils achieve considerable success in these types of involvements, as long as schools have given them opportunities to become so involved *and* have prepared them with the skills to enable them to make these contributions.

(Charlton, 1996b: 42)

Trying out new ideas

As we have shown, strategies for pupil consultation and participation can offer teachers and schools opportunities to look afresh at existing aspects of practice. However, these approaches can also be used to 'break new ground' by offering alternative ways of tackling some of the more pervasive problems faced by schools, such as pupil disengagement with learning, boys' underachievement and truancy. In some cases, individual teachers have initiated dialogues with their pupils to enable them to understand these problems or they have used the insights gleaned from pupil consultation to improve their own practice and to experiment with new approaches.

Innovation can be challenging, however. In exploring new directions for pupil consultation it is important that teachers embark on these initiatives with few preconceptions of pupils' perspectives on the issues concerned. It is also vital that there is a willingness to address pupils' concerns and ideas in a serious and collaborative way. As Cooper and Hyland point out, this approach can offer a powerful dynamic for improving teaching:

> Matters of principle and pragmatism meet when it is recognised that pupils can actively contribute to teachers' developing skills and professional knowledge. The practical justification for enquiring into pupils' perspectives is that their ideas on their school experience are directly relevant to developing more effective teaching.
>
> (Cooper and Hyland, 2000: 22)

The following case studies describe two explorative initiatives – one involves a cluster of primary and secondary schools in a project focused on consulting pupils using role-play and the other is a school's exploration of different ways of consulting pupils about teaching and learning.

Profile 14: The Liverpool Schools Cluster – improving pupil behaviour through role-play (ESRC/TLRP Project, Consulting Pupils about Teaching and Learning)

About the schools

Four Liverpool schools were invited to take part in a special initiative which had twin objectives: one was to look at ways of improving pupil behaviour in the classroom through pupil consultation and the other was to explore the potential of role-play as a technique for accessing pupils' perspectives on teaching and learning. The research cluster group included an infant school, a primary school and two comprehensive secondary schools, all located in Speke Garston, an inner city area in Liverpool that is currently designated as an Education Action Zone. This initiative was part of the Breaking New Ground project (for the ESRC/TLRP Project Consulting Pupils about Teaching and Learning). The group were given advice and support by Phil Freeman, an educational consultant, and the research team from the Faculty of Education, University of Cambridge. The four schools were: Middlefield Community Primary School, Speke Community School, St John Almond High School and St Christopher's Catholic Infant School.

St Christopher's Catholic Infant School provides early years education for local Catholic families in the Speke Garston area. The community served by the school faces many social problems. The school's recent OFSTED report noted that many pupils were entering the school's part-time nursery class with limited language skills and that there were a high number of pupils from socially disadvantaged backgrounds. However, in 2001, the school's endeavours to raise pupils' standards of achievement were recognised by OFSTED and it was awarded the School Achievement Award in acknowledgement of its outstanding improvement.

Middlefield Community Primary School is a new primary school, recently opened following the amalgamation of an infant school and a junior school and, with the closure of another local primary school, the school has seen an rapid increase in its roll with an extra 200 pupil intake. The school's high proportion of pupils who are eligible for free school meals (70 per cent in 2001) again reflects the social and economic hardships of the community it serves.

Speke Community School is a secondary comprehensive school for 11- to 16-year-olds and is currently in the process of moving to new premises. Currently, the school has around 770 pupils on roll and some 63 per cent of pupils are eligible for free school meals, reflecting the high level of social disadvantage in the local area. Strong links with the community are a particular feature of the school and the school has two stated aims:

- encouraging all within our community to realise their full potential
- providing a safe, caring, happy and purposeful environment.

St John Almond High School is a Catholic comprehensive school for 11- to 19-year-olds, situated in a large housing estate in the Garston area. The school has just over 800 pupils, including sixth formers, and an unusual feature of the school population is that there are twice as many boys as girls. It has received additional funding from the Excellence in Cities programme which has been used to set up a study centre for disaffected pupils and those at risk of exclusion.

About the initiative

Phil Freeman, the project coordinator, had extensive experience of pupil consultation and of using role-play techniques to facilitate discussion of teaching and learning. The four schools had undertaken some previous work with Phil and were keen to involve pupils in developing role-play as a way of improving pupil behaviour in the classroom. As a starting point, pupils were consulted on their views of classroom situations and pupil–teacher relationships. It was interesting to analyse pupils' perceptions of teachers and classroom interactions across different school settings. There was clear common ground on some issues: for instance, the question of 'what makes a good teacher' highlighted consensus in pupils' views that a good teacher is firm but fair; has a sense of humour; gives you help when you need it; makes lessons fun and exciting; does not shout; treats everyone equally and gives 'second chances' to pupils who misbehave.

Following these initial consultations with pupils, selected year groups were then asked to work on devising role-play activities based on the theme of classroom behaviour. Each school was expected to contribute a short play to a one-day project conference during which pupils watched and commented on each other's plays and took part in group discussions about the issues raised concerning classroom behaviour. One school added a further dimension to its work by asking a group of Year 10 pupils to take on the role of teacher in a primary school for one lesson. The pupils who undertook this challenge found it a valuable experience and said that it had increased their understanding of the difficult job teachers have and made them appreciate their own teachers' efforts.

Phil Freeman made the following observations on how teachers and pupils had responded to taking part in the research project:

- I was struck by the ease and enthusiasm with which the teachers have taken to the role of teacher-researcher and the lift that this appears to have given to their teaching.
- Pupils have responded with enthusiasm to their involvement in this work: the idea to use role-play has proved to be successful as it allows pupils to explore issues in a relatively non-threatening way.
- During the sessions, pupils developed some transferable skills in areas such as creativity, communication, decision making, co-operative group work, working to aims and deadlines and coping with difficult situations and emotions.
- The use of role-play proved to be a useful strategy, both in terms of the data yielded through the role-play activities and in its contribution to improvements in teaching and learning within the project schools.

The project made extensive use of video-recording and written work (personal logs, surveys and observation notes) as data-gathering and record-keeping techniques and these provided teachers with material for further analysis and discussion with pupils. Some of the recorded data will be used to produce a video that will be used to disseminate the group's research.

Comment

This was a relatively short-term and tightly focused initiative that allowed teachers to investigate an issue which directly impinged on teaching and learning; pupils' classroom behaviour. It was also an opportunity to try out a different way of consulting pupils using the vehicle of role-play. The teachers and pupils who took part clearly found the experience interesting and enjoyable and it has generated interest among other staff in the four schools although they have not yet evaluated the outcomes of the initiative. The development of the role-playing technique may, however, have wider application and there are plans to make a video for other schools interested in using role-play as a consultation strategy.

Another interesting aspect of the cluster's work was the benefit that teachers found in working collaboratively with other local schools, particularly in a project with a cross-phase structure.

Profile 15: Sarah Bonnell School: the pupil consultation 'toolbox' – new ways of consulting pupils about teaching and learning (ESRC/TLRP Project, Consulting Pupils about Teaching and Learning)

About the school

Sarah Bonnell School is located in the London Borough of Newham, an inner city area with a local community that experiences a high level of social and economic disadvantage. The school itself is a popular comprehensive school for girls and is currently over-subscribed. The percentage of pupils from minority ethnic backgrounds is around 80 per cent, with mainly Indian, Pakistani and Bangladeshi girls and some pupils from African-Caribbean, African and Chinese families. The school has had a long tradition of pupil consultation initiatives: it has taken part in the European Socrates Project which drew schools from across Europe into a research programme on school self-review and it was one of the eight schools selected to take part in one of the ESRC/TLRP Network Project, Consulting Pupils about Teaching and Learning projects.

About the initiative

The school had considerable experience of pupil consultation and pupil participation strategies but teachers were interested in exploring new directions for this work. Teachers decided to involve two of its eight Year 8 forms in a focused initiative aimed at developing a 'toolbox' of effective ways of consulting pupils about teaching and learning to support the school's development programme. The forms were selected on the basis that teachers working with these groups would be interested and willing to take an active role in the initiative throughout the two-year project. Twenty teachers who taught these two groups were involved and each was given a project folder containing a log-book to record their experiences and a menu of activities from which to select. Teachers were asked to complete one evaluation activity at the end of every teaching unit and the menu of activities included a range of different techniques from which they could choose, including visual, dramatic, aural and written forms of consulting pupils. In addition to the ideas provided, teachers were encouraged to experiment with strategies of their own. The following were among the techniques used by teachers in different departments to elicit pupils' views on teaching and learning in their subject areas:

- *'My ideal lesson' technique:* Pupils were asked to write about what they thought an 'ideal' lesson in a particular subject would be like. This exercise received an enthusiastic response from pupils, with many offering lengthy, though sometimes unrealistic, suggestions. Teachers who tried this technique felt that it might have been more successful if pupils had been given closer guidance and a tighter structure for their compositions

- *Spot checks:* These were short 'checklists' to be completed by pupils at the end of a lesson and were designed by teachers to give a general impression of pupils' feelings and responses to the lesson.

- *Photo-evaluations:* Pupils were invited to volunteer to take part in this aspect of the research and a group was selected. Each pupil was given a disposable camera and asked to take up to five photographs in one evening or at the weekend about what they felt helped them to learn in the home. The camera was then passed to another pupil. The photos were then brought into class and made into a display. Pupils then circulated around the 'art gallery' and questioned one another about their photos. Photographs proved a very useful way of encouraging pupils to be reflective about their learning in different settings and provided useful prompts for discussion. Pupils also said that they liked having the opportunity to express their feelings visually.

- *Questionnaires:* These were designed and used by teachers in several departments and the questions were focused on specific subject areas. These surveys were found to be a quick and useful method for gathering pupils' views but teachers found that the questionnaire format was an important consideration: in particular, they noted that it was helpful to allocate spaces for each answer so that pupils were encouraged to write an appropriate amount in response to the question.

- *Role-play*: A drama technique was used to explore pupils' perceptions of the classroom as a learning environment (rather similar to the Liverpool Cluster – see Profile 14). Pupils enacted a typical classroom scene, taking on roles as 'teacher' and 'pupils' and these scenes were then used as a basis for whole-class discussion. This role-play technique, which was adopted by several teachers, proved very popular with pupils. Teachers felt that one drawback of the technique was that it required too much time to be used on a regular basis but it was felt to be worthwhile as a one-off exercise.

Comment

Some of the techniques for pupil consultation developed at Sarah Bonnell School proved to be useful ways of gathering information about pupils' views on teaching, according to teachers. Trying out new ideas in this way allowed the project to evaluate whether techniques were effective and practical; some techniques were found to be too time-consuming or unhelpful.

The school's involvement in the project has also given the school opportunities to refine its overall strategy for consulting pupils. As with the Liverpool Cluster, teachers found it helpful to work collaboratively with other schools and the Sarah Bonnell School has taken part in a series of conferences for pupils and teachers from the ESRC/ TLRP Project which included primary and secondary schools from different parts of the UK.

Developing strategies for pupil consultation: some words of caution

Even with careful preparation, firm objectives and clear planning, things can go wrong with an initiative; we have come across some pitfalls and obstacles that other schools may encounter in developing pupil consultation strategies. Armed with words of warning gleaned from other schools' experiences, however, teachers can avoid some of these potential problems in planning their own initiatives. The following themes cover some of the more common difficulties that we have noticed in the course of our research with teachers and schools.

Limited impact

One of the most frequently met problems with pupil consultation initiatives is that they do not fully achieve their objectives or that they have only a limited, short-term impact within a school. This problem tends to arise where, perhaps, the school's expectations have been too ambitious – if insufficient thought has been given in planning and preparing the initiative or if teachers have tried to work to unrealistic timescales and with limited resources. We have often found that when key members of staff leave, or have to take on new responsibilities within the school, pupil consultation initiatives either remain limited to the original focus or department, or they fade out altogether. As Michael Fielding suggests, there is a need for pupil voice initiatives to be given full support within the school, even where only some teachers or departments are involved directly. Fielding writes:

> There have always been gifted and committed individual teachers who have pioneered student voice work in their own classrooms and sometimes in their own schools. But the burden of setting up such approaches and keeping them going, frequently in hostile internal and external circumstances, often proves too much. Even when they do manage to gain some degree of institutional support the initiatives these colleagues create too often founder with their departure or their exhaustion. Hence the importance of systems.
> (Fielding 2001: 105)

Fielding's observation ties in very closely with our own experience of working with teachers and schools but we have also found that schools working collaboratively with others, as part of a wider network or system, can improve the sustainability of their pupil voice initiatives.

Only half the story . . .

Another problem of conducting pupil consultation is that the data obtained from pupils do not represent an accurate or complete picture of pupils' views on the issues under investigation. Gathering data is a complex task and some methods that appear to offer quick, simple solutions (such as closed-answer questionnaire surveys) may not, in fact, yield an authentic account of what pupils think. To help counter this problem it is often helpful to use more than one technique in data gathering and to 'triangulate' findings drawn from the differing methods: for example, issues brought to light in pupil interviews can be followed with a more detailed survey to gauge how widely these views are held or whether they might differ according to age, gender or level of attainment. Conversely, findings from surveys or pupil 'learning diaries' can be investigated through interviews or discussion groups and initial findings may be examined further.

Obviously, *data quality* is a serious consideration and when gathering data it is essential that not only are pupils encouraged to express their opinions openly but that the questions asked will give teachers the information that they need. Careful preparation is essential and piloting interview and survey questions helps to pinpoint any questions that might be ambiguous or difficult for pupils to understand. In questioning very young pupils, particular care has to be taken to ensure that questions are clear. In one case, for example, a simple questionnaire was drawn up by a primary school teacher as part of the school's project on pupils' perceptions of praise and reward and this questionnaire included the following question: 'Who do you like to share your work with?' The teacher was somewhat surprised that the majority of pupils answered 'no one' and concluded that pupils were reluctant to discuss their learning with others. On questioning further, however, the teacher found that many pupils had misunderstood the question and thought it was asking about *working* with other people rather than *telling* other people about their work and their achievements (for guidelines on interviewing and questionnaires, see Appendix 1). It is also important to be aware that young children can be influenced by the interview situation and are more likely to give answers that 'please' the interviewer, particularly where the interviewer is also their class teacher (Dockrell *et al.*, 2000). Ways around this problem include asking children to act as interviewers and involving external researchers.

It is not only the wording of questions that can produce misleading or inaccurate data, however. Limitations of time and resources can mean that only some pupils' views are sought and careful consideration needs to be given to which pupils are involved. Obviously, where only certain groups of pupils are consulted then the data gives only a partial impression and more generalised conclusions should not be drawn. Furthermore, as Fielding points out, we must be wary of listening only to pupil voices which are most readily accepted and articulate:

> To talk of student voice is misleading. Some voices (e.g. middle-class girls) seem to be more willing to speak than others, partly because they may feel more at ease with the way teachers speak about students and with the capacity of schools to understand what matters to them in their daily lives.
>
> (Fielding 2001: 101)

And Fielding goes on to invite us to think about this question:

> To what extent do the perceptions and intentions of students who are most often and most readily listened to reflect the experience of those students for whom school is an uncongenial or alienating place?

Clearly, where there has to be some restriction on the numbers of pupils directly involved in consultation, it is important that no one feels that their voice has been silenced or excluded from the process. Whenever possible, the reasons for selecting groups must be explained to pupils so that they understand why only some have been involved in the consultation process.

The importance of preparing the ground

Before consultation strategies are introduced, it is essential to prepare the ground by making the initiative's objectives clear to teachers and pupils and by creating a positive climate in which everyone involved feels that the process will have some benefit to them and to the school. To enable pupils to feel secure about giving their views, they should be informed about the aims of the consultation and given assurances about confidentiality. Similarly, members of staff who are not directly involved in the consultation should be briefed about what is happening. Care should be taken to make pupils feel comfortable with the data gathering processes: for example, those carrying out interviews should present themselves in a friendly, informal way. Consultation needs to be carried out in relaxed conditions so that pupils do not think of consultation as being part of an assessment process.

A further issue concerning teacher researcher and pupil consultation is the possible effects this process may have on the teacher's role and position. As Kirby points out:

> For teachers involved in research there is a potential conflict between their role as a teacher and that of a researcher. The first is an established position of power, which includes the education and development of young people, imposing decisions and maintaining discipline. A researcher is classically expected to be a detached and impartial observer, encouraging voluntary rather than enforced participation, who records rather than challenges opinions.
>
> (Kirby, 2001: 75)

'Culture shock'

Occasionally serious difficulties can arise as a result of pupil consultation, particularly where the process has not been introduced and carried out with sensitive regard to the prevailing school culture. For example, there have been incidents where teachers who were not directly involved in the initiative have felt threatened by the idea that pupils' views about their personalities and teaching practice were being sought and have raised objections. In some cases, schools have found that pupil consultation strategies highlighted contentious issues and that open discussion of these issues led to hostility in the staff room. However, these problems have tended to occur in situations where there were existing tensions in the school and pupil consultation was not the primary cause of the difficulties.

Conclusion

In this chapter we have looked at a range of different approaches to pupil consultation and participation and considered some of the potential benefits and pitfalls that schools have encountered with these initiatives. Although the words of caution need to be borne in mind, the profiles clearly demonstrate that these approaches often prove helpful for teachers and schools and that they can offer new directions for improving teaching and learning. This chapter has looked at evidence from individual schools and has illustrated the wide variety of ways in which pupil consultation approaches are being developed to improve teaching and learning. In Chapter 3 we take a broader perspective on pupil consultation and consider what we have discovered about teaching and learning through listening to young learners in a series of research projects carried out with schools across the country.

3 Pupils' perspectives on teaching and learning

Learning, like any other achievement in life, is not necessarily an easy or straightforward endeavour and every learner is likely to find difficulties with some aspects, or at some stages, of their schooling. Through consulting young learners about their experiences, we have been able to build up a clearer understanding of the struggles that pupils often have with learning. Evidence from our research suggests that pupils are sharply aware of 'sticky patches' in their learning and that they are often perceptive in distinguishing the kinds of help that enable them to make progress.

Pupil data also suggest that problems experienced by individual pupils can have a ripple effect. For example, fear of 'falling behind', which is a recurrent concern for young learners, sometimes increases a pupil's motivation to work harder but it may, conversely, lead to a pupil adopting other, less positive, means of preserving his or her self-esteem – i.e. through behaviours which have a negative effect not only on the pupil's own learning but on the learning of those around them. In this section we look at pupils' perspectives on things that make a difference to their learning and achievement and at their views of the kinds of resources, systems and strategies they need to succeed.

The term 'learning support' is often used in relation to the needs of pupils who have some specified, and generally long-term, difficulty with learning but 'learning support' can be used in a more general sense to encompass any form of assistance or facilitation. Here we adopt this wider definition in looking at what young learners have said about their difficulties with learning, why these problems may arise and what kinds of support enable pupils to overcome them. Evidence from pupil interviews offers a vivid, and sometimes surprising, picture of the kinds of difficulty that pupils experience in their learning. There were six common themes:

- A question of time.
- Understanding assessment.
- Understanding the criteria for 'good' work.
- The impact of friendships on learning.
- Sustaining pupils' engagement with learning.
- Building a positive identity as learner.

In the following sections we will look at each of these themes in closer detail and consider how pupils' perspectives can help teachers and schools provide more effective ways of supporting learning for all pupils.

A question of time

The rituals of bells and timetables, terms and school years are so familiar to us that we rarely think about why the rhythm of teaching and learning is marked out in this way. The question of time and learning, however, is an important one. In the 1960s American researcher John Carroll (1963) suggested this equation to express the relationship between time and learning:

school learning = f(time spent/time needed)

Carroll explained *time spent* as being a function of two things: *opportunity* (the amount of time made available for learning) and *perseverance* (the percentage of this time that pupils stayed on task). *Time needed* he described as a combination of *pupil aptitude, pupils' ability to understand instruction* and *the quality of instruction*. Though modified in recent years the model's basic premise – that time needs to be considered as a key factor in successful learning – holds fast. Carroll's model relies on quantitative measures but if the question of time is considered using qualitative evidence a rather different set of issues emerges. In the following section we look at what pupils say about the question of time and consider their views on:

- how time is managed within lessons
- the structure of the school day
- the rhythm of learning across the school year
- the importance of making up for lost time.

How time is managed within lessons

In school, time allocated for teaching is largely segmented into lessons and, according to our pupil data, the balance of timing within individual lessons is crucial. In particular, many pupils feel that too much time is spent on monologues of teacher explanation, leaving too little time for carrying out work. Clearly it is important that pupils are given enough information so that they understand what they are expected to do but they also need sufficient time to carry out learning activities. Consulting pupils can help teachers to find out whether or not they are getting this balance right. One primary school asked Year 5 and 6 pupils how they felt about the timing within lessons. In these extracts from the school's questionnaire survey, pupils describe their preferences about the balance of timing within lessons in different areas of the curriculum:

> In science or English I need a longer time spent on instructions and I like it when we go into smaller groups and someone explains it again slowly. (Y5 boy)

> I like a long explanation if we were starting a new subject [like] area, fractions [or] adding but in English I like a short and informative explanation. (Y6 boy)

Pupils also commented on the pace of their work in relation to the boundaries of the lesson:

> In maths I like whizz through it but when it comes to English I press on slowly because I find it harder. (Y6 boy)

> With something hard or interesting I like working slowly but with something easy when we finish our work we get to do something nice. (Y6 girl)

The amount of time a pupil requires for a particular task will vary and accommodating the needs of individual pupils is one of the perennial difficulties facing teachers. When pupils lack the time to complete work or to grasp new ideas, their confidence can quickly diminish. Our secondary school data show that many pupils worry about understanding things properly and about getting 'left behind' and feel that they need more time to think through new concepts and to work on things they find challenging:

> You have to have time, I think to get yourself in – with things like maths and stuff – you're good at it and you know it but sometimes it takes you a little time to click . . . You've got to have time for you to work it out yourself, you know, instead of people saying 'Well, you should know this by now and you should do this.' (Y8 boy)

> If somebody says, like, you have got ten minutes and you have got to do this, you feel more under pressure and you think 'I've got to get this finished.' And then you worry about that . . . (Y8 girl)

As well as needing more time in certain subjects some pupils also struggle because they have to work at a slower pace as a result of their general learning difficulties. For example, our data draw attention to the problems pupils experience in keeping up with the pace during lessons because they are 'slow writers': '[The teacher] sort of fills the board, like, and you're trying to write really fast but I'm a really slow writer and then [the teacher] goes onto something else and it's really hard to understand' (Year 8 girl). We also noted that many pupils – particularly at primary level – think that time has an important bearing on the presentational quality of their written work:

> I would like to go slowly so my handwriting is neater and I can make it look good . . . (Y6 girl)

> I like doing my work quickly but neatly so I get a good mark but I have time to relax at the end. Normally I check my work thoroughly so I need to go pretty fast. (Y6 boy)

While some pupils are concerned because they do not have enough time, those who prefer to work at a faster pace can feel frustrated and 'held back' on occasions when they have to wait for slower pupils. Higher attaining pupils can quickly become bored, particularly when explanations are repeated for pupils who are finding work difficult, as these pupils' comments suggest:

> ... doing speed maths [is boring] because if you are really quick you have got to wait for all the other children to finish writing the questions and then you have got to wait until you have heard the next question and the teacher is usually repeating it. (Y4 boy)

> ... if you're, like, able and you are with lots of people who are unable to do the work then you get dragged behind and you get bored by the work you are doing. It is just like you are not being stretched and 'Oh, right. What is two add two?' (Y8 girl)

As well as time allocated for tasks and activities, pupils say that they sometimes want more time to respond to teachers' questions. Observational studies (Rowe, 1972; Stahl, 1990) confirm that teachers do not always give sufficient time for pupils to think about questions asked in class. An American study (Stahl, 1994) indicates that this issue is an important one and that, if teachers simply extend the 'think-time' with a pause of between three and five seconds, this can have positive effects on pupils' learning. Outcomes resulting from the adoption of the extended 'think-time' approach include increases in the length and correctness of pupil responses; fewer 'I don't know' responses and no answer; an increase in volunteered, appropriate answers by more pupils and improved performance on academic achievement tests. A recent study by Black *et al.* (2002) also emphasised the need to increase the response time for pupils as part of strategies for improving classroom practice:

> Wait time has to be increased to several seconds in order to give pupils time to think and everyone should be expected to have an answer and to contribute to the discussion. Then all answers, right or wrong, can be used to develop understanding. The aim is thoughtful improvement rather than getting it right first time.
>
> (Black *et al.*, 2002: 7)

Another issue pupils raise is the lack of time in lessons to follow up things that interest them or to do extended pieces of work on topics they find fascinating. Many pupils said that they like to work on projects where they are allowed several weeks, rather a lesson or two, to complete their work:

... in a lesson you do something and then the next day you're doing something else and you could really enjoy it but then the next day you forget about it. But if you like go on for weeks you can do something really good on it but if you just did it one day, you've got one piece of work to show for it. (Y9 girl)

I prefer doing projects because I can get really interested in it, rather than just doing worksheets on my own which is really boring. You don't mind doing projects at home because they are a bit more interesting and when you get to school and you can talk to your friends and say 'Look!' and you can put it all together and it is a really good feeling of satisfaction. (Y8 girl)

On the other hand, when teaching moves on quickly from one topic or activity to the next, pupils can feel that their learning is fragmented and piecemeal. This Year 8 boy describes the problem:

Well, like, for ten minutes at the beginning [the teacher] will be telling you what to do and you do it and then they will stop and ask questions or something like that and then start again It's just breaking it up so ... (Y8 boy)

However, pupils spoke positively about some recently introduced initiatives that allow more extended ways of working. For example, these Year 10 and 11 pupils found that GNVQ modules offered them the chance to carry out longer, more continuous pieces of work:

You can concentrate on [modules] rather than thinking 'Well, I thought we were doing this last week and that the week before'. You don't know where you are but when it's a module you know you're doing the same thing until you stop and you go on to something else, so that's good. (Y10 boy)

Well I do GNVQ as well as my GCSEs and I find that better because you can choose. They will give you a task but they won't split it up and say 'Do this Monday. Do this in five minutes, this in fifteen minutes.' You get the chance to split the task up yourself so that if there is something you find difficult, then you give yourself longer for it and the easier things you cut down, so you get it done. You still have deadlines and everything but you meet them in the way you want to. (Y11 pupil)

The pressures of our current school system rarely allow for these less time-constraining sequences of learning activities but there may be benefits in giving pupils greater autonomy in deciding how to use time in the classroom. As this Year 6 boy suggests, allowing more flexibility and self-direction in time management could be helpful for both faster and slower learners:

> Instead of just saying 'Do this and do this and then do this' [teachers] could, like, say 'Do this', and then 'Have you finished yet?' and things like that and then give [us] a bit more time and . . . when someone is finished they could get them to help someone else who is struggling a bit. (Y6 boy)

And, as this older pupil points out, working independently and managing one's time are important skills, both in the context of school and in later life:

> We need more freedom and choice in what we do at school. This would prepare us for work where we have to get a certain workload done before a certain time . . . (Y9 boy)

The structure of the school day

Although timing within lessons is important, pupils' perspectives also suggest that the structure of the school day itself has an influence on learning and behaviour. We noted that even the youngest pupils recognise day-to-day patterns of teaching although they may not use the word 'timetable'. They may be confused about the notion of discrete 'subjects' and what terms like 'geography' or 'science' entail, as illustrated by the comments made by these Year 3 pupils:

> *Girl 1*: We didn't do literacy in Year 2. We do it in Year 3 . . .
> *Girl 2*: . . . because we didn't have literacy when we were in Year 2 or 1.

> I like making houses and things. We're making houses in design and technology – I think it's called design and technology but I'm not sure. (Y3 girl)

The introduction of the National Curriculum and national strategies for literacy and numeracy in primary schools has led to considerable change in the character of primary schooling (Galton *et al.*, 1999) – making it, in some ways, more like secondary schooling. Many schools have introduced more rigid timetables with fixed time slots allocated for different aspects of the curriculum and it has been suggested that pupils now experience a more pressured and fragmented style of teaching and learning (Pollard and Triggs, 2000). Our data confirm that primary pupils are often aware that there is little time to spare in the school day:

> If [the work] is really hard you won't get it done quickly and the teacher would say 'We have got five minutes!' And you don't finish it in time and you waste all your playtime doing it. (Y4 girl)

> I know the answers – I was just, you know, rushing to get it done so I got most of the answers wrong, apart from a few hard ones that I really concentrated on. (Y4 girl)

In the secondary phase, the school day takes on a new character. When they start secondary school, pupils are often intrigued by the different format of the school day, with its sequence of subject lessons and the movement from room to room and teacher to teacher (Rudduck *et al.*, 1996). This Year 11 boy describes his experience of the contrast between primary and secondary school in this way:

> When I was at the primary school it was not like it is [here] where you do all these different subjects . . . I can only remember doing English and maths when I was at primary school, as well as other things but not the subjects we do up here now. I don't think it's anything like it.

Once the excitement of transfer has worn off, however, pupils may be less enthusiastic about this time structure. Some pupils, for example, feel this rapid sequence of lessons makes it more difficult for them to sustain their concentration and our data include suggestions about having fewer but longer lessons: 'There should be fewer lessons and more time in those lessons to cover more work and to go into further detail . . .' (Year 9 boy). And the movement between classrooms is also unhelpful, according to some pupils: 'I'd prefer it . . . to, like, stay in one classroom and not move about too much – like they did in the [primary] school really' (Year 10 boy). Pupils also commented on the need for 'free periods' during the school day that would allow more time for independent study:

> Say if we had a free period and we know that we've got a test or something coming up, we can use that free period as an advantage . . . (Y8 girl)

> Pupils should have time in the library not for any one subject but as study time so they can do homework and use the library resources. (Y9 girl)

Another issue concerning the school day that pupils frequently raise is break times and, surprisingly, given earlier research findings (Blatchford and Sharp, 1994), some pupils feel their concentration is interrupted by break times and they are frustrated by these intrusions if they are working on something important to them:

> Say if you have got to do a piece of work and you are really into it and you are doing really well and then suddenly it is dinner time and you have got to stop and it's just like – if you see what I mean – but it sort of puts you out of your rhythm . . . (Y8 boy)

When pupils are 'switched on' to learning in this way, they may look for more opportunities to work on things that interest them:

> [It would be good] to let us in during lunchtimes [if] we want to do some work in drama or something. (Y10 girl)

However, our data also confirm Blatchford and Sharp's assertions about the value of break times. Pupils see break times as important and enjoyable parts of the school day and value the opportunity to go outside and to engage in unstructured 'play' activities. Primary school pupils' comments suggest that they see break times as being occasions for 'fun', for social interaction and physical activity. The excitement of the playground is evident in the words of this Year 3 girl, who was asked what she found different about being in the junior school:

> The playground's bigger and you get more things on the play-ground from when you were in the infants . . . We have monkey bars, we have wobbly boards, we have a massive chain which wobbles and this big plank of wood and things you have to jump and sit on and a football pitch!

As part of our investigation of pupils' perspectives on being in Year 3 we invited pupils to produce drawings to illustrate what they thought Year 3 was like. It was interesting to note that many of the drawings featured playground activities and friends rather than classroom scenes or learning activities, suggesting that these aspects were at the forefront of pupils' image of school.

The issue of break time, however, also raises a rather different set of concerns. For both older and younger pupils periods of time outside lessons may sometimes lead to problems such as bullying or arguments that can affect their confidence and well-being. Younger pupils spoke of their fears about being in the playground – which included physical harm:

> . . . because the playground is really hard and if you fall over [you get hurt]. They don't want us to get upset and crying and stuff . . . (Y3 girl)

Being rejected or ignored by their peers was also a serious worry for some children. When Blatchford (1998) asked primary school pupils about things they disliked about being at school, some pupils spoke almost exclusively about playground experiences, and being alone was a particular worry.

Break times in secondary schools are quite different in character. Middle and secondary pupils' comments about break and lunch times suggest that boredom is the most common problem:

> There isn't much to do at lunch time, just sit in the Block. (Y8 boy)

Pupils offered some sensible suggestions about ways of improving break time provision:

> [The school council] should talk about getting some more clubs for dinner times. Like, because we've got gymnastics club and netball but sometimes lunchtimes get a bit boring for an hour and the library shuts. (Y10 girl)

And some felt that being given opportunities to expend their energies during break times would help to reduce disruptive behaviour during lessons:

> If it's better at school – if we had more fun – then maybe we would be OK with doing work and stop mucking around so much in lessons. (Y8 girl)

However, our data also show that fears about bullying during break times are still prevalent at secondary level:

> Well, I'm having a few problems with a few bullies. I've tried loads of times to tell them to leave me alone but they don't. (Y8 girl)

> I was probably the person who got the most bullied round here and I think that's what makes me not want to come to school . . . It's over but I mean, like, if it starts again, I'm scared of it happening again. (Y10 girl)

Teachers and schools are well aware of these issues and some have adopted policies of pupil consultation and participation to help remedy break time problems (see, for example, Profile 11: Tany's Dell Primary School). These strategies include peer support systems, positive behaviour schemes and consultation about ways to improve break time provision. Involving pupils in such strategies has proved useful and many schools are developing anti-bullying strategies that give pupils an active involvement in resolving the problem. Langford Primary School in Fulham, for example, has been working with Kidscape (a national charity dedicated to preventing bullying and child abuse) on a peer support approach. The school reports:

> Our 'Bullybusters' club has helped pupils to see that we as adults have taken these issues very seriously and have actively helped to solve these problems. By having their peers involved to help them to help themselves (mentoring), and along with all the other positive behaviour strategies being introduced, we have seen a real improvement to the entire ethos of the school.

Bullying is, perhaps, the most serious 'downside' of having break times. A rising number of American elementary schools are even abandoning 'recess' periods due to concerns about children's safety and the intrusion into teaching time (Pellegrini, 1995). However, studies show that break times are important and can have a positive effect on pupils' learning: for example, Jarrett *et al.* (1998) found that primary age pupils were more likely to focus on learning in the classroom if they had a break time during the day. A few schools in the UK have tried alternative ways of organising break times such as rotating schedules for different year groups to allow better supervision of playground activities and to segregate different age groups.

As well as changes to the timetable and break times pupils also comment about the length of the school day. As might be expected, some pupils believe the day is too long and does not leave them with enough time for sports and social activities, particularly if they live some distance from school. However, there are also calls for some extra time to be added to the school day so that homework can be completed in school and there is better access to help and resources. One Year 9 girl proposed the adoption of the 'early start' day as used in some European countries:

> If we started at 7.30 a.m. we could finish at 12.30 p.m. . . . which means you could have your lunch, do your homework and go out, instead of being too tired to do anything.

Breakfast and after-school clubs are increasingly common in primary schools but these tend to be a facility for working parents rather than an educational provision. At secondary level, optional facilities like study centres and homework clubs have been introduced in many schools but the responses of the pupils we spoke to have been mixed:

> I come to the study centre, cos like indoors (i.e. at home) it's like noisy. Well, it's a wild house sometimes! All my brothers running around and I can't concentrate because there's nowhere I can study. (Y9 boy)

> [Teachers] could help you after school and that but I don't think pupils are that willing to give up their own time and that . . . I can't be bothered with it. It's more work . . . (Y10 boy)

> I've only started coming [to homework club] recently because I realised how much work I had to catch up on . . . but before I just didn't think about it. (Y11 girl)

However, MacBeath *et al.*'s (2001) extensive study of after-school provision suggests that many pupils appreciate after-school support and that this type of provision can have a beneficial impact on pupil attainment. According to the study, pupils find learning in this more relaxed atmosphere has a number of benefits:

It is not the teacher teaching us like at school. We do whatever we feel will help us. (Student, Sarah Bonnell School, Newham)

It has made me more confident and independent. Now I can stand in front of my entire year group and do my speaking and dancing. A while ago I couldn't do that. (Y11 girl, Shirelands Language College, Sandwell)

In recent public debates on education, there have been calls to extend the school day but research from the United States suggests that this measure would not necessarily have a beneficial impact on pupils' learning (Karweit, 1982; Ellis, 1984). A more effective solution to time constraints might be to readjust school structures to permit greater flexibility with time, as Gross suggests:

Present school structures that curtail forward thinking can change. For example, Sizer's (1985) idea of longer class periods has developed into block or intensive scheduling. This alteration of a traditional school structure signals greater belief in learner ability to concentrate for longer time spans and to delve deeper into course content. This change also raises expectations for teachers to learn strategies to make extended sessions exciting, not just more of the same.

(Gross, 1997: 41–2)

The rhythm of learning across the school year

For the majority of pupils 'moving up' from one class to the next in same-age cohorts at the end of the school year is a familiar routine (although mixed-age classes have been introduced in many primary schools in response to economic and practical considerations) and currently most schools are still using the three-term system, dividing the year into three terms of unequal length separated by Christmas, Easter and summer holidays. There have been calls to change this system and the Local Government Association is currently conducting a review of the structure of the school year. The existing structure, introduced in the nineteenth century when some pupils in rural schools had to help at harvest time, has been widely criticised and studies have demonstrated that lengthy holiday periods can impinge on pupils' learning (Cooper *et al.*, 1996). Evidence has been drawn from measures of pupil performance and school inspections and the views of practitioners and parents have been sought but there has been little research on pupils' experiences of the school year.

Our research evidence suggests that, from the pupil perspective, each school year follows a predictable pattern, although it is also apparent that pupils perceive some years as being more 'important' or more challenging than others. The first term is generally seen as a period of 'settling in' when pupils become accustomed to new teachers, new groups and a new curriculum. Some pupils believe that teachers make allowances for them during this period or, as one Year 8 boy explained, 'they're nice to you' at the start of the year. For some pupils starting a new year represents an opportunity to change:

> I want a fresh start . . . I do mess about a bit in some ways but [this] year I think I'm going to do even better and I'm going to try not to mess about. (Y8 girl)

For other pupils, returning to school after the long summer holiday can be an unsettling experience and they may take some time to adjust to new conditions.

Pupils often seem to regard the second term as a period of more 'steady' working:

> . . . you're sort of into a routine by now, when you get to this [term], you are sort of into a routine of what you do in lessons anyway and so you feel happier. (Y10 boy)

For pupils who are in years that include formal assessment (Years 2, 6, 9 and 11), preparation for tests and examinations becomes more intense during this term with more frequent testing or mock examinations. More exciting events – plays, open days and sports events – tend to be held before Christmas or after the completion of summer tests and examinations, leaving the spring term as relatively featureless.

In contrast, the summer term often includes more variety and excitement. Many schools offer opportunities for pupils to experience new ways of learning during this term and these can help to re-engage pupils' interest in learning – as one girl put it,

> The fun things come up just before the holidays. (Y8 girl)

Of course, for some year groups, this time of year is a period of anxiety and pressure as deadlines for coursework, tests and final examinations loom:

> I don't like exams. I can do well in them but I don't like all the lead up to it, cos everyone's pressing you to revise this, revise that but for me revision just doesn't work. (Y10 boy)

However, the end of the year is also marked by celebrations of achievement. Many schools have reward schemes intended to raise attainment, promote more positive attitudes and improve attendance:

> Well, at the end of the year you get to win a certificate if you've got 100 per cent attendance or 99 per cent or 95 and upwards or there's how many credits you've got. (Y8 boy)

Some schools organise open days and sports days to involve parents and the local community in recognising pupils' achievements. Another familiar feature of the summer term is sending home the school report on pupils' progress during the year. Some older pupils comment that the timing of reports is not helpful and they would prefer to be given feedback earlier in the year:

> [We] only find out about [our grades] when at the end of the year we get the reports and then they only put the effort [grade] and the one the teachers put. (Y10 boy)

Our pupil data show that the rhythm of teaching and learning through the school year is still shaped by the long-established pattern of the three-term system. This system is currently under review and it is interesting to note that, although the consultations being carried out by local authorities are seeking the views of practitioners, parents and employers, pupils' opinions on this important issue are not, it seems, widely canvassed.

The importance of making up for lost time

> *Interviewer*: If you could start again from Year 7 would you change anything?
>
> *Year 10 boy*: I'd change everything because it's just been a waste of time really – me being at this school. I've wasted everybody's time.

Although some pupils have difficulty in coping with the increasing levels of difficulty as they move through their school careers, others find that their learning is hampered by prolonged absence or lengthy periods when they have been distracted from work. Some pupils have talked to us about the effects of being absent for a long time, whether through illness, family difficulties or through deliberate choice. A typical problem these pupils face on returning to school is feeling 'out of place' and being made aware of the gaps in their learning which could lead to humiliation or frustration, as these girls describe:

> Because with me being away . . . we have all these tests and that and all French words for, like, bread and stuff like that and I don't know any . . . Well, when you get something wrong they all start laughing at you. (Y8 girl)

> I'm struggling a bit with [coursework] because I don't really know what we're meant to do. Everyone's like wading through it because . . . I were absent and they've been, like, explained to and other people what didn't come to the lessons . . . [the teacher's] not explained it to them. (Y10 girl)

Some also spoke candidly about how their own disruptive behaviour in school had led to them falling behind with their learning and how it appeared to them that the difficulties they now faced were almost insurmountable, as this Year 9 boy explains:

> *Pupil*: I am not paying enough attention because last year I were in trouble a lot with [subject] so I didn't get to learn much, I just kept sulking and not paying no attention and it has all come back on me this year.
>
> *Interviewer*: Do you think you will catch up in that subject?
>
> *Pupil*: Oh, no. I'm far too behind. (Y9 boy)

However, our data suggest that the problem of catching up on lost ground remains a low priority and in too many schools there are no systematic procedures to support pupils who fall behind in this way. The project 'Improving Schools – The Pupils' Agenda' invited primary and secondary to schools to describe strategies that they were developing to support pupils who needed to catch up in their learning (this theme was one of three key issues explored in the project) but only a few schools volunteered information on strategies to help pupils who had missed work. The pressures of classroom teaching often mean that pupils who have been absent do not receive the immediate help they need to enable them to get back into the swing of things. There were some schools, however, where pupils, particularly in Years 10 and 11, have been given customised support to help them to catch up with their learning and these strategies – including homework clubs, one-to-mentoring, revision and 'catch-up' sessions and personal counselling – have proved successful in many cases (for further details see the report, *Improving Learning – The Pupils' Agenda*, 1999).

It is during the last two years of compulsory schooling that pupils tend to become most sharply aware of the effects of lost or wasted time in previous years. Some have adopted the attitude of this Year 8 pupil:

> When I get in the upper school, I think that's the most important years of being at school. The first and second year I don't think is too important but it is important when you get, say, to the third and fourth year. (Y8 girl)

In Year 11, however, these pupils find that they lack the foundations of learning now needed to achieve the qualifications they want. Some reconcile themselves to working harder as the final examinations or coursework deadlines draw nearer, hoping that last minute efforts will improve their chances of success:

> I've made a resolution I'm going to work after the holidays . . . I've managed to dodge quite a lot of work recently so I've got to catch up. (Y11 boy)

In many cases, resolutions like this one are not kept and these pupils leave school with few or no formal qualifications. The sense of regret about wasted time is clear:

> ... when we were in the fourth year we use to muck about and not get on with work. We used to sit talking and that. Like the fifth year when it were all due to end ... tomorrow never comes and then – 'Oh, me exams! I haven't revised!' (Y11 girl)

> I missed loads of school work which was my own fault and I'm suffering from that now ... I thought 'Oh, it doesn't matter. I can make up the work' but I didn't. I don't know what we're doing so it's a waste of time now. (Y11 boy)

There was a common feeling among older pupils that, although support is important and can improve their chances of success, ultimate responsibility for achievement lay with themselves. A Year 11 boy, who had received a great deal of support from teachers, explained that some of his friends were not willing to respond to teachers' efforts in the way that he had:

> A couple of me mates, they've had loads of support – it's just the teachers ain't getting none back off them. [Teachers] can't do anything. It's up to them now and they're not doing nowt. Me mate got suspended the other day and they let him back in and he's been mucking about again. (Y10 boy)

Conclusion

As Holloway and Valentine suggest, the structure of time in schools is very largely adult-directed:

> Children spend most of the weekday in a very time-disciplined environment at school where all their activities from arrival, registration and lessons, through to eating and playing, are governed by the daily rhythm of timetables and bells which signal the choreographed mass movements of pupils within the school.
>
> (Holloway and Valentine, 2003: 108)

However, when we look at pupils' perspectives on these structures it is apparent that time is an important factor that can give rise to a range of problems. Some pupils seem to find it easy to 'catch the beat' and stay up with the pace of teaching and learning but, for others, keeping in step is harder because they need to learn at a faster or slower rate. Our pupil data highlight some interesting issues concerning the question of time and this evidence suggests some ways in which existing time structures could be modified, including:

- allowing longer 'blocks' of time for activities and lessons
- giving pupils greater autonomy in deciding how to balance their time on tasks
- ensuring that pupils have sufficient time to answer verbal questions
- offering more opportunities to work on long-term projects
- providing time and space for independent study, within school time and outside
- supporting the development of pupils' time management skills.

Understanding assessment

Assessment is an aspect of teaching and learning that often stirs the emotions and confusion about its nature and purpose is not wholly confined to pupils. Our evidence suggests, however, that many pupils do not see assessment as being generally supportive of their learning and progress but rather tend to think of tests, marks and grades as being finite measurements of their ability and potential. Unless the rationale for assessment practices is explained, pupils may give less attention to teachers' comments than to the given grade (Butler, 1988). A study of Year 3 by Doddington and Flutter (2002), for example, found that the way that testing was explained to pupils could make a profound difference to their confidence: for instance, in some schools the tests seemed to make children 'very conscious of what they could *not* do rather than what they *could* do', while in other schools pupils were quite clear about why they were given tests and seemed to understand that testing was to help them make progress in their learning. The following extracts suggest that younger pupils were able to see tests that were part of ongoing teacher assessment in a positive, constructive way – although the first comment suggests that tests are accepted as a means of dividing pupils:

[Tests] are probably because teachers want to see how good we are and probably put us on a higher table. (Y3 boy)

> I think [tests] are good because they can tell your next teacher how good you are and what sort of things you know and what sort of things you need to work on. So that's tests. That's what you learn from. We learn from our mistakes. (Y3 boy)

Pupils' responses to teacher assessment were different from their responses to more formal assessment such as Standard Assessment Tests (SATs) and GCSEs that often give rise to anxiety and stress. It was apparent that, in both Year 2 and Year 6, the national SATs loomed large in pupils' minds and, particularly in Year 6, we noticed that some pupils felt that their learning was almost entirely focused on achieving good grades in the SATs. One Year 6 pupil, for instance, described his school day in this way:

> When we come in, in the morning, the work we're going to do is on the board. When we get to the lesson [the teacher] will explain what it is and what we're going to learn and she'll also explain why we need to do it because it might come up in the SATs. (Y6 boy)

The feelings expressed by this pupil were shared by many other Year 6 pupils we spoke to and it was clear that they were aware of teachers' own sense of pressure. These observations are confirmed in the investigation of primary pupils' perspectives on teaching and learning, carried out by Andrew Pollard and colleagues, the Primary Assessment, Curriculum and Experience (CASE) project. The PACE researchers noted how pupils' responses to formal standardised testing varied and that their responses often linked to the school's way of approaching these tests:

> Some [pupils] were fortunate in attending schools that had created secure, non-threatening climates and enjoyed peer cultures that were conducive to learning. In such circumstances high attainers began to feel more confident and even exhilarated during the test period. However, we have also seen how other pupils, particularly low achievers, found it hard and could not cope. Under pressure they became de-motivated and dysfunctional as the difficulty of the SAT challenges overwhelmed them.
>
> (Pollard and Triggs, 2000: 238)

Further evidence of negative effects associated with national testing is provided by Galton *et al.* (2003) in their recent investigation of primary head teachers' perspectives. This study found widespread concern among head teachers about the impact of Year 6 SATs on pupils' confidence and on their attitudes to learning.

Negative responses to assessment are not restricted to younger pupils, however. Secondary school pupils interviewed in our projects tended to see assessment as a measurement of their ability rather than attainment and they seemed to feel that grades and marks effectively defined their potential.

Processes like target setting, which are intended to help pupils improve the quality of their work, are similarly problematic and tend to be seen by pupils as yet another form of assessment, this time defining in advance their chances of success. Rather than giving pupils an idea of how they are performing and what they need to do to improve, targets can appear to be just another obscure hurdle. As this Year 10 girl's comment suggests, target grades are often presented to pupils with little further explanation:

> No one has ever talked to me about the targets . . . like, no one has ever told me how I can reach that target . . . (Y10 girl)

As other pupils at the same school said, knowing how to improve was more important than vague instructions to 'do better' or 'work harder':

> Rather than just set the grade, at the end of the day that may be what you have to aspire to but rather than just doing that they could point out the areas where you could really do with improvement rather than just sending round a piece of paper with like . . . profile grade, target grade and efforts and things like that that don't mean anything. It's what you need to improve on that should be there . . . (Y10 girl)

> I'd find it helpful if someone were to just sit down and talk through say, like, you could get a C by doing more revision or, like, do more coursework or just writing a bit more . . . like my science teacher said to me 'If you'd revised a bit more you'd get more in your grades' because that's like something that lets me down, I don't revise . . . (Y10 boy)

Such comments raise the question whether formal assessment has actually contributed to an improvement in pupils' learning. The Assessment Reform Group's recommendations offer an alternative basis for constructing an effective system of assessment. The group proposes that

> . . . improving learning through assessment depends on five, deceptively simple, key factors:
> - the provision of effective feedback to pupils;
> - the active involvement of pupils in their own learning;
> - adjusting teaching to take account of the results of assessment;
> - a recognition of the profound influence assessment has on the motivation and self-esteem of pupils, both of which are crucial influences on learning;
> - the need for pupils to be able to assess themselves and understand how to improve.
>
> (Assessment Reform Group, 1999: 15)

Understanding the criteria for 'good' work

Our data suggest that pupils do not always understand what teachers mean by phrases like 'You must try harder', and 'This work is not good enough.' These are familiar phrases in classrooms everywhere but there is often a mismatch between what teachers intend to convey by using these phrases and how pupils actually interpret it. These misinterpretations can have serious and long-term implications for pupils if they feel that their efforts to 'try harder' and to produce good work are unrecognised and fail to meet the required standards.

Younger pupils, in particular, think that working hard is about being quiet, producing a larger quantity of work and completing work on time. This Year 3 boy's remark is typical:

> I think it's good because I did it quickly and kept to the deadlines.

They also tend to assess the quality of their work in superficial ways such as its neatness and its having 'no rubbing out':

> I take [my creative writing] for homework and do it in neat and take a lot of time, use a guide line. If I go wrong I try again. (Y4 boy)

It was surprising that older pupils held quite similar views: for example, working harder was often taken to mean talking less in the classroom rather than applying concentration and effort to the task in hand and there was also a parallel concern with presentation rather than content:

> Well, if I look back at my book and I find my handwriting's neat and my drawings are better and like it's set out better then I'll find I could praise myself because of that. (Y8 girl)

Our data suggest though that the criteria for 'good work' are not always explained clearly enough and pupils are sometimes disappointed when the mark they are given for a piece of work does not reflect the effort they put into it. And when a piece of work is returned covered in a teacher's red-penned comments and a request to redo the work, then pupils are likely to feel upset and discouraged:

> I feel angry, sad – she's told me to do it again. (Y3 girl)

> If I copy [my story] up and Miss says it's not good enough I might be a bit upset . . . (Y3 boy)

Self-assessment and self-evaluation offer alternative approaches to assessment and have some advantages, as Valencia and Bradley suggest:

> We have viewed learning as the students' job, assessment as the teacher's job. Yet, unless students are part of the assessment process they will fail to take ownership, interest and pride in their learning, and we will have failed to 'hook them'.
>
> (1998: 175)

Our data suggest that where pupils assess their own work, effort and time taken are generally foremost in their evaluations and their sense of pride and accomplishment are very clear:

> This was probably one of the first pieces of work [a drawing of a butterfly, part of an art project] that I have actually ever bothered to sit down and for five minutes persevere at it. I'm very proud of it. (Y8 girl)

> . . . some people in my class had to finish their escape story for English and I had a page and about a half to do in just a single

lesson – that is forty minutes, and I thought I can never do this and then I didn't talk to anybody, I didn't stare at anybody, I just concentrated and I wrote it down in my neat book and I got it done. I felt pretty surprised and I thought, at the beginning, I am never going to do this and I was surprised that I did it. (Y5 girl)

Effort and time, however, were not always enough to ensure a good mark or grade and a frequent problem was that pupils did not fully understand how to improve the quality of their work. For example, pupils spoke of their uncertainty about when a piece of group work in drama was of a high enough standard or whether their research for a history assignment had covered enough ground. When these uncertainties arose, pupils tended to compare their own work with that of others in the class although this did not always prove to be a helpful strategy as other pupils might, of course, be equally unclear about what was expected. A more effective strategy was for teachers to discuss the criteria of good work with pupils as part of an ongoing dialogue about learning. As Paul Black and colleagues propose, it is important for teachers to consider

> . . . the quality of the responses that [they] make, whether in dia-
> logue or in marking homework. Effective feedback should make
> more explicit to pupils what is involved in a high-quality piece
> of work and what steps they need to take to improve. At the
> same time it can enhance pupils' skills and strategies for effective
> learning.
>
> (Black *et al.*, 2002: 20)

The impact of friendships on learning

Few teachers would disagree that, for pupils, the social dimensions of classroom life often take precedence over the academic. Pupils of all ages tend to find that peer relationships often exert a powerful influence on their feelings of confidence and self-esteem, on their attitudes and behaviour and also on their learning and performance. While bullying and difficulties in sustaining social relationships are obvious concerns and can have a profound impact on pupils' well-being, there are also issues concerning friendships that have consequences for pupils' learning and achievement.

Our data include extensive evidence of the positive dimension of friendships and suggest that they are an important means of support, particularly for pupils who are experiencing difficulties with their learning. The influence of friendships seems to vary, however, from direct support with work to a more pastoral one. Direct learning support from friends was referred to by pupils across the school age range. Sometimes friends explain things in a way that is easier to understand and it is often quicker to ask a friend for help than to wait for a teacher. Indeed, as Pollard and Triggs observed, in the primary phase pupils spend the majority of their time in the classroom working without teacher interaction and therefore have extensive opportunities to work with other pupils:

> Just one-third of children's classroom time was spent in some form of interaction with the teacher or other adult – leaving no less than two-thirds remaining where pupils were either alone or interacting with other children. This is a consistent pattern and provides a clear indication of why friendships and peer relationships are so significant to primary pupils. Having friends to share work with and to talk to is vital to accomplishing each day in the primary classroom.
>
> (2000: 57)

However, as the following comments demonstrate, pupils at both primary and secondary stages recognise the value of friends' support with learning in the classroom:

> I'm sitting next to Jane and she helps me if I'm stuck and I help her. Sometimes she helps me know the answer but she doesn't actually, like, say 'Oh it's 36', she says 'Well, how many tens has it got . . . ? Now count the units . . .' (Y3 girl)

> Like in maths I sit next to [girl's name] and it's good fun – if I don't understand something [the teacher] kind of ignores you and I just say to [girl's name] 'How do you do this?' and she explains it and things and we try and help each other if we don't understand things. (Y8 girl)

> In technology and engineering teachers have control but they let students talk to each other to help. Some students find it easier to

get help from friends instead of teachers so, instead of just sitting in silence and doing work, they need encouraging. (Y10 boy)

On the other hand, working with friends could also simply make classroom activities more enjoyable and interesting, adding a social dimension to learning that encourages pupils to regard these activities as 'fun' and exciting. Opportunities to work collaboratively are generally popular and pupils feel that working in this way can help them to produce better work. Sometimes working with friends just makes an activity seem more stimulating:

... because when you have to find things out, like in history or geography, you work with friends in doing it and that makes it quite fun. (Y4 girl)

In other instances, working with a friend can have a more direct impact on the success of a task:

We're working in pairs so if one of you is better at music and the other is better at IT, if you can work in pairs you can combine the two. So it ends up that you both learn off each other because usually you end up with friends who'll have different kinds of skills. (Y8 pupil)

This Year 8 girl also explains that friendships can help to create a positive learning environment and this was an idea that many other pupils, particularly in this age group, shared:

A lot of teachers think you can't concentrate when you are with your friends but it is a more relaxed atmosphere. We work better in a more relaxed atmosphere.

There were also some indications that peer relationships could provide a very direct stimulus to pupils' progress: this Year 10 boy, for example, explained how his motivation and engagement with learning was enhanced by the competitive edge of peer relationships:

Pupil: But friends is [sic] important though, isn't it?
Interviewer: Could you tell me about that?

Well, it's because, like, say you sit next to them and they're doing lots of work. You think 'I've got to catch up to them' so you start working faster and better. You want to beat them. (Y10 boy)

Friendship, of course, is not always a positive factor and friendship groups, both within and outside the school, can have a detrimental influence on pupils' learning. Teachers and pupils were well aware of the problems associated with friendships but, for pupils, there was a clear tension between their need for social 'acceptance' and their desire to do well at school. Middle and secondary school pupils admitted that their friends were likely to distract them from concentrating and interrupted their work. Some pupils said that they were often drawn into disruptive behaviour because it would impress their friends and it created a 'cool' image for them among their friendship group. Like many other pupils we spoke to, these two pupils – a Year 10 boy and a Year 11 girl – said that their attitudes to work at school reflected the culture of the peer group and that this contributed to their lack of engagement with learning:

> It's just, like, I think the people I hang around with are really lazy and don't want to work. Might be to do with that I suppose . . . (Y10 boy)

> I just never do any work hardly. I just can't be bothered to do it. A lot of the group don't do anything . . . (Y11 girl)

Pupils differed in the extent to which they were susceptible to peer group pressures and, for those who were strongly influenced by the negative attitudes of friends, these pressures could make it very difficult to change from a disruptive 'messing about' image to one of a hard-working, conscientious learner. The nightmare scenario for some pupils was becoming labelled with the much-hated term 'boff', as this Year 8 boy's comment suggests:

> I don't want to be in the top group . . . if you're in the top group you've got a good chance of getting a better job but if you are in the top group at school you get called a boff so . . .

Some found that having acquired a 'troublemaker' image it was equally difficult to escape from the reputation they had gained with teachers. In rejecting negative peer influences, some pupils found that their attempts to change their image and re-engage with learning were hampered because they had been put in teaching groups with other pupils who did not want to change their attitudes. This Year 11 boy, for example, felt that because of his established image as a trouble-maker, he did not have an opportunity to escape the consequences of his previous behaviour:

> So now I'm in a group where other people like that are [i.e. disruptive] and most of them just mess about so you can't really do any work anyway because work's right easy. They [i.e. teachers] don't expect a lot of you. (Y11 boy)

For disruptive pupils who wanted to get back into learning, it was not only their image with friends and teacher that raised problems. These pupils often felt acutely aware that there were gaps in their learning and were frustrated when their attempts to make up for lost time were obstructed by other pupils' antics, as this Year 8 boy explained:

> I get in arrears a lot, see . . . I don't look forward to going to [subject] because I know that it is, like, noisy in there and sometimes when I want to be good, just because they are so noisy it does my head in so I start shouting. (Y8 boy)

Nevertheless, some pupils continued with the struggle to change their image; they tried to make up for lost time and some found that it was possible, with support, to get back into learning. Avoiding the distraction of friends often remained difficult but, when pupils were sufficiently engaged by learning activities, their interest and sense of involvement enabled them to focus on their work. This Year 8 boy explained that he needed to be kept fully occupied in order to avoid the distractions of friends:

> Also if you're bored you are going to be dumb. You're going to do something stupid, you're going to try and show off or something like that. But if you're – if you're doing some work then you're going to be concentrating on the work not trying to show off to your friends or being dumb or something. (Y8 boy)

Those pupils who were able to break out of the 'anti-learning' images that their friendship groups had sustained appreciated the opportunity that teachers had given them to change their ways. This Year 11 boy described the changes that had resulted from being given a second chance by his teachers and from being separated from the negative influence of a disruptive friend:

> When I went with him [best friend], like, it were only me and him and, you know, on my reports and stuff from the second year teachers were telling us to split up because we were messing about. And after he went I made – bit by bit – I've made a bit more progress like, you know. Now most of my friends are messing around a bit but they work hard as well and they set a good example for me so I work hard as well. But before, with him, we just used to mess about . . . (Y11 boy)

Apart from distraction and disruption, friendships can also have a damaging impact on pupils' learning and confidence when they go wrong and friends split up. For younger pupils, the loss of a friend or membership of a social group can be a devastating experience. In our work with Year 3 pupils, for example, we found that this issue was a very serious concern for many young learners. The move into Year 3, as we have suggested, marks a period of change and upheaval for many pupils: some were transferred into junior schools on separate sites and, even for those in primary schools, there were often changes in social groupings (some schools, for example, had separate playgrounds for Key Stage 1 and Key Stage 2 pupils). As pupils coped with these transitions, the social aspects of the classroom became a paramount concern. Some felt anxious and upset when they were separated from the close friends that they had made when they were in Key Stage 1, as illustrated in these comments from Year 3 pupils:

> I didn't think it was fair because I had [always] been with my best friend in my whole life. I've been in her class all the time and she went to [another class] and I was disappointed and sad because I've been with her since I started school. (Y3 girl)

> I miss some of my [Year 2] class. We are splitting up and some of them are in [another] class and I miss them and I will only get to see them at break times. (Y3 girl)

Borland *et al.*'s study of the middle years of primary schooling confirmed the prominent role played by friendships in shaping pupils' social and emotional development. They conclude that 'Involvement in friendships which are going well seems to be crucial to children's sense of emotional well-being and self-confidence. Hence, when they went wrong, they were a source of pain' (Borland *et al.*, 1998: 100).

Our evidence supports this conclusion but we would also argue that, as well as the affective issues identified by Borland and colleagues, friendships affect pupils' academic success in school.

Secondary school pupils who were less confident about aspects of their learning sometimes said that they needed friends to give them support with their work. Setting by ability often involved splitting up friendship groups and for some pupils this separation could lead to a loss of practical help and confidence, as this Year 10 girl explains:

> Well, my friend got dropped out of the top set so I have to sit on my own now and the work is really, really hard and I've, like, asked if I could go down to the second set but [the teacher] said no first time. She said I weren't getting out of it and then I think she's talking with Set Two teacher to move me down and I hope I can move down because then I'll enjoy school a lot more because I dread Mondays and Thursdays because of [those lessons]. (Y10 girl)

However, as they progressed through secondary school, it appeared that many pupils became increasingly self-reliant and autonomous and, as the final years of compulsory schooling approached, there seemed to be greater resistance to the influence of peer group pressures. While these changes in peer influence have frequently been noted in psychological studies of adolescence (for example, see Brown *et al.*, 1986; Coleman and Hendry, 1990) it is interesting to see that pupils themselves are conscious of their increasing independence and value their autonomy as a step towards the world beyond school.

Data from our pupil interviews and from other published research studies (Roffey *et al.*, 1994) also suggest that pupils often have quite a sophisticated awareness and understanding of how friends affect their learning. For example, it was interesting to note in our interviews with pupils that many could make a clear distinction between friends who helped them in some way with their learning and those whom they enjoyed being with but who were likely to have a negative effect on their work. Even quite young pupils could make this distinction, as these comments from pupils in Years 3 and 4 suggest:

> I work best with Holly doing maths because she doesn't mess about and if I sit with Tom he always jumps up and take the book all over the place. (Y3 girl)

> Well, I find when you sit with your friends sometimes . . . if you sit with too many of your friends you don't work very well so it is best to just sit with one or two of your friends . . . (Y4 girl)

> Sometimes when it is hard for your homework and your mum is too busy I sometimes ask to see if my friends can come round to help me and I find that easier. (Y4 boy)

Being given a choice about who you work with was generally liked by pupils. Their decisions were often based on sensible criteria rather than seen as opportunities simply to gather together and chat. Many pupils said that they found their work improved when they could work with pupils they got on well with – as one Year 7 pupil explained:

> [In drama . . .] you can also go with sort of friends instead of, like, your worst enemies in the class because . . . Well, they make you work in drama but you still have fun. I mean, I think everyone has fun in drama but you still work hard at it.

Our data underline the powerful impact of social relationships on pupils' learning and achievement both inside and outside school. However, pupils' accounts raise some important questions about how teachers can support the link between friendship and learning; they are, understandably, often more concerned about the problems that arise through pupils' social interactions in the classroom. There is a need to look more closely at the benefits of supportive friendships, whether through formal strategies like peer support programmes or indirectly, in allowing pupils some degree of choice in grouping and working arrangements. The role of friendships is a double-edged sword in the classroom and, as we have seen, it may serve, or sever, pupils' engagement with schooling – but it can also support the improvement of learning.

Sustaining pupils' engagement with learning

> If it's more exciting it helps you to give it more of a try, like, give it a real go . . . (Y4 boy)

> If you enjoy it you tend to try harder. It is just something that happens naturally. (Y8 girl)

Engagement with learning, as the words of the two pupils above suggest, is an important source of motivation but it is not simply about 'entertaining' young learners or making lessons 'fun'. In a recent comment to the British Press (*The Times*, 17 January 2003) about the French system of education, Luc Ferry, the French Minister of Education, described his own childhood experience of schooling as excruciatingly dull, saying that he, and some 80 per cent of his fellow pupils, during their years in the classroom, had been: '. . . as bored as dead rats'. Surprisingly, he was not using this analogy to argue the need for lessons today to become more exciting but proposed, instead, that pupils should expect to 'endure' rather than be inspired by their experiences in the classroom. This idea that learning is, of necessity, an uninspiring and tedious process runs counter to the idea that people learn best when they are motivated and engaged with both the purpose and the process of learning (McCallum *et al.*, 2000). While there is a consensus that pupils learn best when they feel a sense of engagement, the factors involved in sustaining pupils' interest and motivation are less clear. In listening to young learners we have been able to identify some factors that can make a difference to pupils' engagement with learning.

One issue that pupils frequently raise when discussing lessons that they find stimulating is the variety of activities. There are constant references to boredom when pupils felt that lessons are not presented in imaginative ways and when learning activities are limited to a repetitious format of worksheets and textbooks. For some pupils creative, 'hands-on' ways of working not only helped them to understand difficult concepts but also engendered a sense of achievement, particularly when this was a tangible 'end product'. These pupils in Year 8, for example, explained their feelings about practical work:

> If it's a creative thing, like making something or projects are better than just sort of copying from the board because you can actually feel you've accomplished it when you finish it . . . we get work sheets and copy off the board or dictation – you don't feel like you have accomplished anything. (Y8 girl)

> I enjoy music much more when it's like this – practical stuff. It's better than learning about scales, theory, copying stuff, doing worksheets – but you kind of have to learn that before you can do

all this. You probably could learn all that off the computers but we didn't have computers when we started. Since we've had the computers we haven't really done much of that. It's much more interesting like this. No matter how many worksheets you look at, you don't know what it sounds like. (Y8 pupil)

Having opportunities to make choices in the classroom was also identified by pupils as having an impact on their engagement with learning and their sense of ownership. Pupils of all ages spoke about their sense of pleasure when they could make decisions about their work:

I think I would choose free [i.e. creative] writing because I like to let my imagination go wild. You can, say, have like a three-headed monster or there's like this beautiful castle . . . you can pretend you're in Africa, India or Australia or anything you want to be . . . because it really unlocks your ideas if you're doing free writing because then you can just relax and let all your ideas pour out onto the paper. (Y4 girl)

I like to be set projects that you can do within a certain number of weeks, say two weeks. You have got to produce a piece of work, so this means you go home and do lots of research, spend as much time as you want, space out your time, organise yourself and it is self-driven. I like that. (Y8 boy)

Understandably, pupils wanted to feel that the work is interesting and also useful. These two pupils – one in primary school and the other at secondary school – clearly felt that the work they were doing was not sufficiently purposeful:

Having to write about things like how old I am . . . it's really boring and I already know and so do other people. I can't see the point of it. (Y4 girl)

Well, really most of the homework I've got is really just quite pointless stuff. I mean I did do the stuff that I really needed to. Like if I had an end of term essay that needed to be done I'd do that, but any little sheets that I already knew . . . (Y8 boy)

Many pupils also spoke of their dislike of work that seemed to be going over 'old ground' and they did not understand the need to consolidate their learning with further practice in skills that they already felt confident about, as these primary school pupils commented:

> I know all my handwriting skills now and it is just like we are going over the same things over and over again and I just don't need the extra help with handwriting because I can do it all now. (Y4 girl)

> Well [it's boring] when you don't learn a lot and you're just doing things that you've already done. Just going over and over. Like you keep doing spellings and things that you've already done. (Y6 pupil)

Repetitious and 'easy work' has a clear negative impact on most pupils' engagement with learning and they are quickly switched off learning by activities that they think of as a waste of time. A sense of challenge and novelty are important as these comments from pupils in a Year 4 class suggest (all were from the same primary school):

> I think that if there is something hard and it is like new, when I have never done it before, then I think, 'Yeah, I want to do this!' but sometimes if I have thought, if I have done it before and it was easy and I would go, 'Oh, I don't have to do this work' . . . (Y4 boy)

> I like a challenge. It's much funner [sic] than doing something you have already done. (Y4 girl)

> I like doing things really hard. I think if you do easy things once you have done them it is sort of easy and if you do very hard things, it is more of a big challenge and you can see how good you can do and try and do better than you have ever done before, doing something very hard. (Y4 girl)

And this Year 10 boy contrasted the interest inspired in one subject, where he felt a sense of challenge, with another in which he felt unchallenged:

> *Interviewer*: You don't think you get enough challenge?
> *Pupil*: Yeah. I am in some [subjects] but in things like history that's challenging because with the questions they ask you can go into quite a lot of depth about them, depending on how much you want to but in some of the subjects, like IT, there isn't no challenge really' cos there's nothing really at the end of it. (Y10 boy)

However, the challenge must not be too distant or destabilising. There is a fine line between challenge which discourages and challenge which excites pupils to work at a new level:

> As long as you have got something to work towards which you know you can achieve within the level then I think you will enjoy the lessons more. (Y9 pupil)

> Like if we're doing Year 9 work but we're only in Year 8 because the teachers think that we could do it and that just makes it more difficult when we're used to doing Year 8 work and we're only just getting used to that. (Y8 girl)

An interesting strategy, developed by teachers at Brooke Weston City Technology College in Corby, Northamptonshire, allows pupils to work at a level they feel comfortable with and yet challenged by. The four levels, which are linked to the National Curriculum standards, are known as 'basic', 'standard', 'extended' and 'advanced', and tasks in each lesson are matched and assessed according to these levels. Pupils work in mixed groups and can choose to move up or down a level if they wish, although teachers may offer advice if they feel a pupil is not choosing wisely. These comments, made by pupils during interviews with our project team, suggest that the self-selecting strategy, supported by opportunities for self-evaluation, can have beneficial effects on pupils' attitudes to learning:

> You feel peer pressure to go on and do extended because you want to come across as being as good as [other people] are . . . (Y10 pupil)

> [Here] you have to evaluate your work and see if you can do better and I find that better because you will be learning from your mistakes, not always being told what to do because in life, let's face it, you're not going to have someone telling you what to do all the time. You've got to, like, take charge and you've got to be independent . . . I think that this school does start, at a very young age, giving you independence, doing what you want to do, like with the basic, standard and extended. (Y10 pupil)

In the course of our research in other schools, however, it was apparent that pupils' engagement with learning could be undermined

– especially by the emphasis placed on written work. Writing was something that many pupils found problematic across all Key Stages. Boys' difficulties with writing have been confirmed by national performance data (compiled by OFSTED and by the School Curriculum and Assessment Authority) and in published research studies (for a review of recent research see Arnot *et al.*, 1998) but the factors underlying the figures remain unclear. Although this issue has been widely researched, the reasons for pupils' difficulties with writing are not fully understood and our data offer some further insights into why many pupils find that the quantity of written work affects their engagement.

One of the most common difficulties with writing that pupils referred to in interviews was that they did not have the dexterity required for writing legibly and they were embarrassed that they did not write as neatly as others. Pupils said that they struggled with the physical effort of writing and this appeared to be more commonly a problem that affected boys. It was interesting to hear boys' perspectives on their difficulties with writing and the wider effects that these problems have on their learning in general. Lessons that involved too much writing were more likely to switch boys off learning, as the Year 8 boy's comment suggests:

> You just think 'Oh another boring lesson', you know. More writing. Because you know exactly what is going to happen – you are going to go in, you are going to get told off, you are going to have to sit there, copy from the text book. (Y8 boy)

It was clear, however, that classroom activities that did not involve writing were more likely to engage pupils' interest and pupils said that they liked tasks that were 'different' or involved some degree of physical movement, as evidenced in these two comments from secondary school pupils:

> [I like it when you can] go to all different rooms and you don't have to stay in one classroom and just copy everything out. You can go on the computers and copy things out on that. It made it more interesting than having to write. (Y8 girl)

> Sometimes the teachers give you like games to do and you don't realise it but it does help you a lot because in maths the teacher gives us some games sometimes and, sort of, just a

piece of paper and you work in pairs and it is OK sometimes. (Y7 boy)

Conversely, classroom activities that carry on for long periods without physical movement can reduce pupils' engagement with learning:

[I don't like] reading the book on the carpet because it is really boring and . . . You wait and wait until the others have corrected their spellings and all we are doing is sitting on the carpet, reading our books. (Y4 girl)

It's just like having to sit there for a whole hour just doing work and there's no pattern to it, apart from drama, there's no like get up and doing things. Just sitting there, doing work, that's what you're doing five hours of the day. (Y10 girl)

For many secondary age pupils, engagement with learning is also linked to their perceptions of the kinds of knowledge that are required for life in the world outside the school gates. Having a relevance to these 'real life situations' makes topics seem more interesting:

[In] English I find it hard to learn and concentrate because it is boring and uninteresting. I think it needs to be more exciting and involve more topics that concern us, that we can relate to and find interesting. (Y10 girl)

Interviewer: What do you think the school does at the moment to support your learning?
Pupil: The teachers . . . the way they do everything. They make the lessons interesting because if it's interesting you pick more things up so it's easier.
Interviewer: In what ways do they do that?
Pupil: They don't just tell you the facts that they expect you to deal with, they put it into context, like real life situations . . . (Y10 boy)

Relevance to future life or employment opportunities could influence pupils in determining which subjects they were prepared to work hard at and which they would reject as 'pointless'. While subjects like mathematics and English were almost universally regarded by pupils as important, pupils' responses to other areas of the curriculum reflected personal interests or constructions of importance:

The fact is that I have worked well in the subjects that I consider to be of any practical use to me. I mean I just think of it that way: that if I'm ever going to practically use this I need it and I need to learn it now. But if I might practically use this once every year or something there's no point. So, like with languages you wouldn't necessarily think 'Oh, yeah I'll be in France 99 per cent of my time so I've got to learn French'. I just won't. (Y8 boy)

Another factor influencing pupils' sense of engagement with learning was receiving positive feedback and encouragement from their teachers. Most pupils felt that praise was an important source of motivation and would share the view put forward by this Year 10 boy:

Pupil: The teachers motivate you when you're in the lesson quite a lot actually.
Interviewer: Can you explain how?
Pupil: Always giving you encouragement and telling you to do your best, things like that. Trying to make you achieve more really . . . (Y10 boy)

Even the more confident learners seemed to need reassurance that they were making good progress on a regular basis. Some pupils, however, did not rely on teacher feedback to motivate them and it was their own sense of pride and competence that provided the impetus to go on trying to do better. This Year 10 boy explained how the opportunity to put previously learned skills into practice helped to give him a more positive outlook on his GCSE coursework and encouraged him to do his best:

At the moment, for me, it's me coursework. It's started in most subjects and that's actually helping me more than the actual lessons we'd had because it's given you that chance to put everything you've learned during the year into practice . . . (Y10 boy)

Many pupils found that the conditions of learning in school were not fully conducive to learning: for some the home environment was seen as better. More confident, independent learners were keen on working at home because they could work autonomously. Sometimes pupils simply liked being away from the distractions of classroom life:

I like working from home because you can space your time and you can spend as much time as you want on it . . . and you don't have the hassle of class life, say like having to do it in a certain time, so you can spend time on it. (Y8 boy)

I like to work at home if I'm doing lots of writing because you get lots more time without having to be disturbed. (Y8 pupil)

It was evident that disruptive behaviour often had a devastating impact on their learning. This Year 10 girl, for example, described how her work had been affected over a long period of time by the behaviour of other pupils; her despair is evident as she explains the dilemma:

I've told my mum how I feel, how I can't get my work done, and the other day in maths because the teacher was arguing so much with the pupil, because the pupil were just shouting back at the teacher, I just walked out and took me stuff with me and saw my Head of Year and she said go and work outside the tutor room and it's been going on since last September and I've just had enough. (Y10 girl)

In some cases, teachers have used pupil consultation as a way of finding new ways of dealing with disruptive behaviour in the classroom and have invited pupils to participate in developing schemes that reduce the incidence of such problems.

Of course, one reason why pupils turn to disruptive behaviour is that they are bored; their attention is not focused on learning and there is a dangerous circularity in that disengaged pupils' behaviour leads others to switch off learning because they feel that there is little point in trying to work under these conditions. Pupils can also switch off when they need help but don't get it. These two Year 8 pupils' words illustrate the sense of bored resignation that could set in whilst waiting for help in the classroom:

If they give you sort of work that you can't do and they try to explain it to you and you still can't understand it and you can't do it and you just sit there and do nothing. (Y8 pupil)

I'd just give up. I'd feel there's no point if the teacher's not helping. (Y8 girl)

In waiting for help or resources, pupils can indulge in non-learning activities which disrupt the lesson and disturb the work of other pupils.

In considering the pupils' perspective on things that make a difference to their engagement with learning, we have shown that pupils are often highly perceptive about the factors that shape their work at school. What they have said about the conditions of learning in school may not always surprise us but, in listening to their perspectives, we may be able to concentrate our efforts on improving those aspects of schooling that can make a difference. Among the issues that were identified in our data as affecting pupils' engagement with learning were the following issues:

- Pupils of all ages like to feel a sense of challenge in their learning but they also want to feel that they can cope with the demands placed on them.
- Learning activities that offer variety and novelty increase pupils' sense of engagement with learning and, conversely, work that is considered repetitious or mundane tends to switch pupils off.
- Having a sense of ownership of their work in the classroom can promote pupils' engagement with learning.
- Pupils often appreciate opportunities to take more time, and to go into further depth, with topics and subjects that they are particularly interested in.
- Older pupils tend to take a more serious approach to their learning when they perceive subjects and topics as having relevance to everyday life and as being important for their future lives.
- Frustration and boredom can quickly set in when pupils find their learning is obstructed, for whatever reason, and that they are therefore prevented from making good progress.
- Variety in lessons helps to sustain pupils' engagement with learning.

Building a positive identity as learner

Consulting pupils has enabled us to investigate how they respond to the conditions of learning they experience in school but has also served to highlight the differences between individual pupils in the kinds of difficulties they encounter and the extent to which these difficulties affect their achievement, whether in the long or short term. The 'external' aspects of the school environment clearly play a large part in shaping pupils' attitudes and performance but these represent only half the picture of why some pupils succeed and others do not. We have already examined how the pace of learning can present a diverse range of problems to pupils; the kinds of difficulties that some pupils experience with understanding the 'specialised' language of the classroom; and the question of why some pupils fail – for a variety of reasons – to develop a strong sense of motivation and engagement with schoolwork.

In response to these issues, some schools have been looking at ways of improving the conditions of learning to raise pupils' achievement and in Chapter 2 we reviewed some strategies that have been introduced to support pupils' learning. However, there is also an 'internal' dimension to the question of how to raise pupils' standards of achievement and this requires giving attention to the personal feelings and perceptions pupils hold about their abilities and capacities as learners. In an extensive psychological study of pupils' perceptions of the factors causing academic failure, Al-Methen and Wilkinson (1992) found that in early adolescence pupils tended to attribute their lack of success at school to both external and internal factors including:

- their difficulties in coping with assessment (including the format of tests and examinations)
- the lack of relevance and personal satisfaction with the subjects and topics being taught
- their personal feelings and self-perceptions (such as anxiety, fear of failure, poor self-image) and attitudes (including things like a lack of concentration and being distracted)
- problems associated with teacher behaviour and pupil–teacher relationships
- difficulties with their home and families (for example, lack of facilities and family support with their learning).

Our evidence, gained through listening to the pupils' perspectives on their experience of schooling, underlines the importance of the factors identified by Al-Methen and Wilkinson. In this section we consider why some pupils may hold negative self-concepts and why they tend to regard learning as something that is not 'for them'. We also look at what schools might be able to do to help.

Pupils' confidence in their abilities as learners is linked to their general level of self-esteem and it has long been recognised that the problem of low self-esteem is closely linked with underperformance in school. Research has indicated that the reasons why some pupils develop a poor self-image are complex and are likely to include factors outside the school gates (Rutter and Madge, 1976). Al-Methen and Wilkinson's third point – that pupils' personal feelings and attitudes have a profound impact on their learning – reminds us that we need to gain a better understanding of how these perceptions develop and how they shape pupils' identities as learners. In talking with pupils, we have an opportunity to gain some insights into the factors that shape these self-perceptions.

One interesting issue in our interview data was that pupils often said they did not have enough opportunities to talk to someone about their learning; when they are given these opportunities they found the experience valuable. They like to discuss their problems and progress in private on a one-to-one basis or, sometimes, they prefer to talk about their learning with their parents and a teacher. These Year 5 and 6 pupils felt that they wanted both their parents and teachers to talk with them about their work:

> ... when you have had parents' evening or something like, after they could sort of send you letters so you get the good things and the bad things then your mum or dad could help you improve that and if you don't they can improve that at school and then send a few more letters or have a talk over the 'phone. (Y5 boy)

> I would like to go to parents' evening with the teachers at their desk and my mum and dad there and me because then I would like my mum and dad to hear what the teacher has to say about me. If I need to improve on something, if I need, I don't know, less chatting or something instead of embarrassing me maybe in front of the class ... I would prefer them to tell me out of the class, you know ... (Y6 girl)

Older pupils also appreciated talking to others about their learning and it was evident that having a chance to reflect on their work and achievements could help to restore their confidence.

An effective strategy for tackling low self-esteem and lack of confidence has been mentoring; this is increasingly common in schools, particularly as a way of supporting pupils who are in the final years of secondary schooling. In some schools one-to-one mentoring has been carried out by teachers or other adults but in a few cases older pupils have been trained in mentoring skills so that they can provide a mentoring service to younger pupils (see, for example, Profile 7: Kesteven and Grantham Girls' School). We found that mentoring was mostly seen by pupils as a helpful strategy; it appeared to be most effective in cases where it provided direct, specific guidance on particular areas of work:

> It's good because in English I get my words muddled up, like B's and D's the wrong way round. Ever since I've been with [my mentor] she makes me feel a lot more confident about it. (Y7 girl)

Other pupils referred to the general effect of mentoring on their confidence in lessons, as this Year 7 boy, who had been part of a peer mentoring scheme, commented:

> I used to be scared of putting up my hand and saying something and now I'm not as scared. (Y7 boy)

There were also mentoring schemes providing support for pupils who had difficulties that were not directly related to teaching and learning but which, nevertheless, had an impact on their lives in school such as bullying, family problems and behavioural difficulties.

Although lack of confidence and low self-esteem presented problems for some pupils, a small minority appeared to suffer from the converse position – an abundance of misplaced confidence that often proved ill-founded. These two Year 11 boys seemed to be self-assured but, according to their teachers, they were unlikely to perform as well as they had predicted:

> All I do, like, in lessons I talk to my mates and then before any exam I'll revise my socks off . . . shock all the teachers . . . it's brilliant! (Y11 boy)

> . . . my strength is in last minute revising before a big exam. I think I'll achieve the same now as if I'd actually worked hard in lessons for the past four years. (Y11 boy)

These unrealistic self-appraisals can pose serious problems for pupils because they tend to lose their confidence rapidly when they realise that they are not being as successful as they had expected. A strategy that proved to be particularly effective in picking up on pupils' overly optimistic evaluations and helped to identify those who were investing minimal effort was target setting, where pupils were asked to set their own targets and talk these through with teachers (see, for example, Profile 6: Rivington and Blackrod High School). This strategy required close monitoring by teachers, however, to ensure that the targets pupils set themselves were clearly defined and useful and that the pupils understood the process and took it seriously. In thinking about their targets pupils were able to identify the reasons why they were not doing well and what they might need to change. These included more effort with homework; catching up with missed work; more revision; paying more attention during lessons and allowing less distraction from friends.

It is interesting to note that these reflections include recognition of factors that arise 'within' the learners themselves – evaluations of their concentration, motivation and effort, as well as 'external' issues finding certain topics and subjects more difficult, a lack of support to overcome problems with learning, coping with the disruptive behaviour of others and balancing time, particularly with social life outside school.

While schemes like target setting, mentoring and one-to-one support are often effective strategies in increasing individual learners' confidence in their abilities to learn, it is evident that school culture and ethos, at a broader level, can also play a key role in shaping pupils' self-perceptions. In visiting schools where pupils were regularly given opportunities to take an active role in the life of the school we observed that this sense of responsibility seemed to heighten pupils' participation. Pupil participation strategies, such as school councils, and pupil involvement in planning and decision making, can help to create a positive learning culture in which pupils feel they are listened to, taken seriously and respected. Ariadne Schemm and her colleagues at the Department of Educational Psychology, Teachers College, University of Nebraska have been looking at ways of enhancing adolescent engagement in learning and decision making and their findings highlight the importance of giving pupils a voice in school matters that concern them:

Students should become active participants in all problem solving and decision making that occurs regarding academic or behavioural programmes. The opportunity to participate in problem solving with teachers and other adults may provide adolescents with the opportunity to take responsibility for academic progress and appropriate behaviour, offer more information about their academic and behavioural issues, and experience school in a more positive light.

(Schemm *et al.*, 2000)

We have come across a wide range of schemes involving pupil participation and we have often been able to discern some of the effects these approaches have on pupils' attitudes and self-perceptions. The school council is a familiar strategy but, as we have seen, the impact of school councils can be somewhat limited insofar as the agenda is often focused on non-learning matters and the council membership tends to be taken up by pupils who are more confident. For those who were not school councillors, the work of the school council was frequently regarded as irrelevant and its role often dismissed as ineffective. In some cases, however, the school council was given an extended brief and its work did have a wider impact on the whole school community. For example, the school council at Sharnbrook Upper School and Community College has a 'Students as Researchers' programme which explores aspects of teaching and learning and reports back to teaching staff. Pupil-researcher Beth Crane from Sharnbrook described how this programme had helped to change pupils' views of themselves and of their roles in school: 'They came to feel like a more valued and respected resource, and to recognise the fact that they were actually an education knowledge base' (Crane, 2001: 55).

Other pupil participation initiatives have included pupil-to-pupil support schemes in which older pupils were given training to support younger pupils who were experiencing difficulties with their learning. These schemes often appeared to have a beneficial effect on both the supporting and supported pupils. In the project Improving Learning – The Pupils' Agenda (supported by the Nuffield Foundation, see Appendix 3) our research team visited a number of schools where initiatives were in place for pupils to support other pupils with aspects of their learning. The project's final report concluded that these approaches were effective in improving pupils' self-esteem. In several cases, the team noted that the mentored and mentoring pupils valued and enjoyed the experience and that the scheme helped to create a more positive climate for learning in which pupils felt secure and supported – and that standards would be improved. The sense of accomplishment and satisfaction of being a mentor is evident in this comment from a Year 10 pupil:

> You just talk to them and get to know them really well and you try and encourage them and get them interested . . . it makes you feel good when you know you've helped someone younger.

Primary school pupils have also taken part in peer support strategies; these were found to be useful for all concerned and it was remarkable how astute these younger learners often were about the potential benefits of working in this way. A Year 6 pupil summed up his views on the advantages of taking part in a peer tutoring scheme for reading with Year 3 pupils:

> You are also helping yourself when you teach someone . . . you are kind of teaching yourself at the same time.

Encouraging pupils to develop a sense of responsibility for their learning and to regard themselves as valued members of a learning community are effective means of enhancing pupils' self-esteem and confidence. However, another important aspect of pupils' experiences of schooling that has a direct impact on their identities as learners is receiving positive feedback and praise from teachers and parents. The issue of praise and reward is a recurrent theme in pupils' comments and it is clearly an issue that closely affects pupils' learning and achievement, not only in terms of its impact on their engagement with the process of learning, but also in its influential bearing on how pupils see themselves and how they assess their capabilities as learners.

Surprisingly, however, our research indicates that there is little consensus among pupils on how praise and rewards should be given. While some pupils were generally quite pleased to receive tokens such as merit badges and reward stickers, others felt that these were trivial and demeaning, particularly at secondary level, where reward schemes were often derided as being 'only for boffins'. These two Year 8 girls, both at the same school, described how uncomfortable they felt about receiving public recognition for their achievements at school:

Pupil: Well, I did a science award. I got my award and we had to get it in assembly and I don't like going up in assembly and getting stuff in front of everybody. I don't mind if they [teachers] tell me in my book or something but not in front of everybody.
Interviewer: Why is that?
Pupil: I just feel weird. You just feel like you're really brainy and it feels like you're pulling your mates down. (Y8 girl)

Interviewer: When you do a good piece of work do you like to be given praise and rewards by teachers?
Pupil: No, because people call you names and say 'Oh she did this', and 'She did that' and I don't like it because people just stare at you and say 'She's always doing that. She always gets mentioned.' I don't like it when they do that. (Y8 girl)

Age was an obvious factor influencing pupils' responses to public forms of praise and, as the comments by the two Year 8 girls demonstrate, there is often a tangible sense of embarrassment among older pupils when they are singled out for special commendations, whether in the classroom or in whole-school assemblies. Nevertheless, there was a widespread acceptance of written forms of commendation, expressed by pupils of all ages, and they said that they liked such things as letters of congratulation which were sent home for parents to read, positive comments written on their submitted work and words of praise and encouragement given in their yearly reports. For pupils who were less confident about their learning, or for those who had made an effort to change their behaviour, this positive feedback often gave a powerful incentive to sustain their efforts. As Bar-Tal points out, however, there is a need for teachers to think carefully in giving comments to pupils about their work and progress because their words can have a powerful influence on pupils' self-attributions. He argues that it is particularly important that effort as well as achievement is acknowledged by teachers so that pupils do not pick up the wrong messages about their performance:

Teachers should directly refer to effort attribution in the case of pupils' success or failure. In either case, pupils should be told that effort is the cause of their outcome. Such information should not be provided only as feedback, but also it should already be emphasised in the instructions that success on achievement tasks will depend on exerted effort. In addition, praise and criticism following pupils' performance should not be applied indiscriminately. Pupils should be especially praised after success on a difficult task which implies that they tried hard and have ability.

(Bar-Tal, 1982: 193)

Our data also show that while many pupils were reticent about being given praise in front of other pupils in the classroom, they generally did want their families to hear about things they had achieved at school and it appeared that passing this feedback onto parents, and other family members, effectively reinforced its positive impact. Interestingly, pupils of all ages wanted to share their achievements with their families and the pleasure they derived from this is evidenced in the words of these pupils:

> *Interviewer*: How do you feel when your parents say 'Well done'?
> *Pupil*: Really happy and it makes me feel I can do better. (Y1 girl)

> I got two stars and one smiley face on my work and I showed it to my mum and she said 'Brilliant!' (Y3 girl)

> . . . my granddad is an artist and I showed [my drawings] to him and he was very pleased with it and the marks I got for them. (Y8 girl)

One Year 10 pupil seemed to be frustrated that his parents were not told about things that he had done well but only informed about his failings:

> The only communication between parents and teachers, apart from the parents' evenings, is in the planners and the only comments that are ever written in there are bad comments – if we've forgotten the homework, never any good comments. (Y10 boy)

Although positive reactions from families were clearly supportive, pupils' comments also drew attention to some ways in which home influences could be unhelpful to their learning. Teachers are, of course, aware of the difference that having a supportive home environment can make on a pupil's achievement in school but pupils' perspectives on family involvement presented a surprising range of difficulties that could affect pupils at any stage of their schooling. In some cases, parents' views on pupils' performance were clearly at odds with teachers', as this Year 5 girl's experience suggests:

> My mum is always pestering me to write neater but my teacher says I write fine at the moment . . . I try to make my mum happy but sometimes I can't . . . (Y5 girl)

In situations where teachers and parents were at loggerheads about a pupil's work and achievement pupils were sometimes left feeling confused and uncertain about their own abilities. Some pupils, who were more confident and autonomous learners, said that they did not like parents 'interfering' in their work and felt that their families sometimes obstructed their independence in learning. The kinds of difficulties pupils encountered with parental intervention are illustrated in the following extracts:

> When I try to do things at home, when [my parents] help me, when I write my stories I say 'No I don't want you to help me for a little bit. I just want to try on my own.' (Y1 boy)

> Well, I don't really like my mum helping me but if it is quite easy I like to do it on my own but I have got three sisters and brothers and every time I try get [my work done] they all barge in, [saying] 'Oh I know the answer to that! I know the answer to that! (Y4 girl)

> My family would help me if I ask them to but I don't like to ask them to because it's *my* work. (Y10 girl)

Another form of parental intervention affecting some pupils was the sense of pressure they felt when their parents took too great an interest and concern in their performance at school. This sense of pressure from parents seemed to increase markedly in the final years of schooling although many pupils felt that their parents did not understand the work they were doing at school and so were applying pressure in ways that were inappropriate and unhelpful. The extent to which this pressure affected pupils' attitudes to learning varied, however. Those who were more independent and confident learners tended to reject their parents' intervention and preferred to maintain their sense of autonomy while those whose confidence in learning was more fragile seemed to be overwhelmed by parental expectations that were unrealistically high. Some pupils needed extrinsic sources of motivation to keep them on track in their learning and therefore they appreciated the impetus that parental interest and pressure gave them.

Our evidence confirms that parental influence and support have a marked effect on pupils' attitudes to learning and on the development of their identities as learners. In particular, pupils' comments have enabled us to see how family influence can undermine pupils' chances of success in ways that are quite subtle and difficult for teachers to spot. For example, some parents only expressed concern about their child's performance in the particular subject areas that they regarded as important and this selective interest could affect pupils' motivation to do well in these subjects:

> Like English, maths and science they will put pressure on me to do well in and then some of the other subjects which they don't think that you really need to learn – like maybe art, music – they won't put pressure on me at all. (Y9 pupil)

Similarly, pupils could feel less confident in their abilities to do well in a particular subject because their parents had little knowledge or skill in this area and therefore they could not offer to help with homework. The homework club, or after-school study centre, has also been an effective strategy for helping pupils who experience problems with homework due to lack of support, resources or working space at home.

Although our evidence includes references to some well-documented problems associated with family background, there were also indications of ways in which the family could play a positive role in developing pupils' identities as learners. For instance, some older pupils described how their families' interest had helped them to feel more confident at school:

> Perhaps saying 'What have you done at school today?' sounds a bit patronising but [asking] 'What have you been doing today?', rather than just at school, you know, [taking] a general interest in your life and that gives you sort of confidence to work. (Y9 pupil)

Sometimes it was simple things that families did that seemed to make a difference:

> When you come home from school there always lots of jam and cakes – called Jaffa Cakes – and I like that. That makes me work hard. (Y1 girl)

Direct parental involvement seemed more prevalent in the primary stage when many parents were taking an active part in pupils' learning, including listening to their children read, helping with homework, attending school events such as sports days and joining in with school trips. With older pupils parental involvement tended to take a more indirect form although there were a few pupils who said that their parents helped with homework or applied some pressure to ensure that they were doing their best at school. Generally it seemed that older pupils preferred to be more independent in their learning but, as we have seen, most pupils appreciated some parental interest and support, particularly when they were facing up to the examination pressures of Years 10 and 11.

Although encouraging parental support and involvement can be problematic for schools our data highlight the valuable role that parents can play in supporting their children's learning. We observed that strategies involving a 'three-way' dialogue for pupils, parents and teachers to talk about learning could be particularly helpful. These strategies included homework planners with spaces for parents, pupils and teachers to comment on the pupil's progress; pupils attending parents' evenings; open days for pupils and teachers to talk about the work they had been doing; and induction events where pupils and parents were informed about changes they would experience on entering a new year, Key Stage or a new school.

However, it is also important that schools have systems in place to help pupils whose families take little interest in their education. This Year 9 girl missed out on important information about her GCSE options because her parents did not want to attend an options meeting at her school:

> *Interviewer*: Did you get along to the Options Evening?
> *Pupil*: No. My mum and dad couldn't come.
> *Interviewer*: And you didn't want to come?
> *Pupil*: I was going to come but I felt stupid coming on my own.

Our evidence suggests that the family can exert a positive influence on pupils' identities as learners and that opportunities to discuss learning with parents and other family members are beneficial. For pupils whose families are unsupportive, however, strategies like Bullock and Wikeley's *Personal Learning Plans* (2000) can be useful in giving pupils the chance to discuss their learning on an individual basis.

The factors that shape and colour pupils' identities as learners are complex and some clearly lie outside the school's sphere of influence and, therefore, teachers may be able to do very little to ameliorate the intractable problems faced by the most seriously disadvantaged young learners. Nevertheless there are many strategies that schools can use to help pupils to develop positive identities as learners and to strengthen their confidence and self-esteem. Exploring pupils' perspectives on the things that make a difference to their self-perceptions and feelings can provide teachers and schools with a valuable tool, enabling them to identify and address some of the key issues affecting pupils' learning and progress.

4 Pupil consultation – what's in it for schools?

Throughout this book we have been looking at how teachers and schools are using pupil consultation and participation to help improve practice and we have shown how pupils' perspectives can be used to gain insights into the things that affect their learning and progress. Clearly, there are many pragmatic reasons for schools to involve pupils in efforts to improve teaching and learning: pupils are able to offer first-hand evidence about teaching and learning; engaging pupils in a learning-focused dialogue can help to support their learning and help build a more positive learning climate within a school. However, pupil involvement also holds a deeper significance for schools because it offers the possibility of taking school improvement efforts beyond the 'quick-fix' solutions often proposed by policy makers and returns schools' attention to what really matters – pupils and their learning. As McLaughlin *et al.* suggest, the pressures on schools have been enormous:

> The educational system has undergone radical reform in the last decade. The reforms have increased the openness to scrutiny and accountability of schools, as well as prescribing the curriculum. In addition, the idea of competition between schools has been implemented.

But, as they observe, in spite of these conditions, '[it] is clear that children still want to be listened to and value it enormously and many teachers still want to listen primarily to the child's voice' (1999: 100).

Perhaps the most important argument for listening to the pupil voice lies in its potential for providing schools with directions for constructing a better future. This transformational potential of pupil voice lies in two dimensions:

- in changing our constructions of pupils and the pupil role
- in initiating change in the structure of schools.

In this concluding section we consider how the pupil voice movement supports school improvement by **making a difference to pupils** and **making a difference in schools**.

Making a difference to pupils in school

In this book we have shown how pupils' perspectives may help to improve teaching and learning in schools. However, the potential benefits of pupil consultation lie not only in what pupils say about their experiences in the classroom but also in what they have to say about themselves and their aspirations. As we have suggested elsewhere (Rudduck and Flutter, forthcoming), pupils' perspectives indicate that the agenda for improvement may need to be set within a broader context.

One point that emerges quite strongly in our pupil data is that young people's experiences of life outside school often contrast sharply with their experiences within school. These differences can give young people the impression that school is a 'world apart' and therefore what happens in the classroom is seen, to some extent, as irrelevant. Some young people have greater autonomy and responsibility at home or in part-time employment and these experiences contrast sharply with their roles as pupils in school. Many find their personal interests, experience and capabilities are not recognised or valued in the classroom. As Wade and Moore point out, the problems arising through this disparity between life in school and outside can be serious: 'Even the most recalcitrant pupils want to learn, though the lessons they actually receive may be an anathema to them' (1993: 43). The problem of relevance has long been recognised but, as many commentators have observed (for example, Watson and Fullan, 1992; Warsley *et al.*, 1997; Arnot *et al.*, 2001), schools are organisations which are particularly resistant to change. Writing over thirty years ago, a 15-year-old schoolgirl said: 'Schools usually have one thing in common – they are institutions of today run on the principles of yesterday' (quoted in

Blishen, 1967: 7). In spite of decades of government intervention and reform, pupils today might still agree with Blishen that learning in school seems to amount to 'being told what to do and how to do it' (1967: 10). Although young people's lives have clearly changed in many ways, schooling continues to be based upon conceptions of childhood that regard young people as dependent and incapable (Lloyd-Smith and Tarr, 2000; Wyness, 2001). However, as Sarason suggests, there is a need not only to change our ways of thinking about children and young people but also to develop a deeper understanding of the learner role:

> One can alter curricula, change power relationships, raise standards . . . but if these efforts are not powered by altered conceptions of what makes [pupils] tick and keeps them intellectually alive, willingly pursuing knowledge and growth, the results will be inconsequential.
>
> (Sarason, 1991: 163)

It is also important that we recognise and respect young people's need for autonomy in learning and imbue the pupil role with a stronger sense of independence. As Gersch argues, schools should confer greater responsibility on pupils for their learning:

> It would seem important to construe children as 'active learners' who need to know about psychology, learning theory, learning processes, memory and behaviour change, so that at the end of the day pupils can take increasing responsibility for their own conduct and plans.
>
> (Gersch, 1990: 129)

Another important aspect of listening to pupils' perspectives is that this process allows teachers and schools to develop a clearer understanding of pupils' responses to schooling. As Lloyd-Smith and Tarr suggest, the pupil voice allows practitioners to gain access to pupils' constructions of teaching and learning:

> . . . the principal justification for giving children a voice in educational policy, in monitoring and quality assurance as well as in research, is epistemological. The reality experienced by children

and young people in educational settings cannot be fully comprehended by inference and assumption. The meanings that they attach to their experiences are not necessarily the meanings that their teachers or parents would ascribe; the subcultures that children inhabit in classrooms and schools are not always visible or accessible to adults.

(Lloyd-Smith and Tarr, 2000: 61)

Information from pupils not only provides a valuable resource for helping practitioners to discover 'what works' in the classroom but also enables them to refocus on learners and their learning. As American researcher SooHoo suggests, exploring pupils' perspectives enables practitioners to put teaching and learning back in the frame:

Somehow educators have forgotten the important connection between teachers and students. We listen to outside experts to inform us, and, consequently, we overlook the treasure in our very own backyards: our students. Student perceptions are valuable to our practice because they are authentic sources; they personally experience our classrooms firsthand . . .

(SooHoo, 1993: 386)

Giving young people more opportunities to say what they think about schooling and developing their sense of responsibility as members of a learning community represent moves towards a different construction of the pupil role. Rather than being seen as dependent and incapable, pupils are regarded as individuals possessing the right to be heard and to be respected as well as the responsibility to act in ways that align with the best interests of their school community.

But how can involving pupils be used to initiate change in schools? Here we look at what schools stand to gain by listening and responding to the pupil voice.

Making a difference in schools

The advent of the 'marketplace' approach in educational policy has led to the creation of a different model of the school which Bonnett describes:

The concerted attempt radically to change the culture and ethos of the school into something akin to a commercial business enterprise has at its heart the identification of pre-specifiable outcomes (products) which meet the requirements of those that education is to serve (the customer). This is accomplished by an edifice of quality checks and procedures to ensure that 'delivery' occurs in the most cost-effective way . . .

(Bonnett, 1996: 28–9)

The notion of customers in education, referred to by Bonnett, is problematic and generally, under the market model, it has been parents and employers whose requirements are regarded as the most important as 'customers' or 'consumers' of educational provision. Schools may, in their broad structures, not look different but there has been a fundamental change in the social and political climate in which schools operate and this has had some ramifications for how schools work and for pupils' experiences of teaching and learning. The pupil voice movement represents a new departure because it is based on the premise that schools should reflect the democratic structures in society at large. Under this conception the school becomes a community of participants engaged in the common endeavour of learning. Similarly, where the pupil voice is attended to, learning comes to be seen as a more holistic process with broad aims rather than a progression through a sequence of narrowly focused performance targets. Pupil participation supports a view of learning that accords with the vision of educational priorities proposed by the European Commission: 'The global objectives of learning are threefold: personal fulfilment, social inclusion and active citizenship. Learning also plays a fundamental role in fostering employability' (European Commission, 2001: 34).

Our profiles of schools' initiatives include several examples of strategies for pupil participation as a means for developing a more democratic and inclusive school ethos. As we have argued, the pupil voice movement bears a particular relevance to citizenship education and enables schools to put the principles of democratic participation into action. Consulting pupils about teaching and learning and giving them a role in decision making represent first steps towards the creation of schools as 'learning communities'. As Hart points out, this is an important development because it allows schools to give pupils some experience of two fundamental aspects of citizenship – responsibility and membership:

> There are a number of important ways a school can influence the development of children as democratically competent and responsible members of society:
>
> - The nature of teachers' relationships with the children, including the way rules are set and discipline is administered
> - The extent to which the curriculum allows for decisions to be made by children and encourages collaboration with others
> - The extent to which children are involved in the government of the school
> - The extent to which the curriculum is related to the daily lives of the children and their community
> - The relationship of the school's democratic structures to the democratic structures of the surrounding community
> - The content of the curriculum.
>
> (Hart, 1997: 57)

As the European Commission's White Paper *A New Impetus for European Youth* (2001) proposes, there is an urgent need to increase young people's participation in the process of change both within and outside the school system. The White Paper urges member states to adopt strategies that promote and support the active participation of young people at all levels – in their schools and communities and in the political systems of their own countries and the EU itself:

> Participation requires young people to acquire skills or improve existing skills. It involves a gradual learning process. The first stage, generally in their own environment (school, local district, town, youth centre, association, etc.), is crucial. It gives them the opportunity to gain the self-confidence and experience needed to reach the subsequent stages. Moreover, in the local community in particular, participation can bring about changes which are tangible, visible and verifiable. At this level young people also have

the chance not only to give their opinion but also to be involved in decision-making processes.

(European Commission, 2001: 23)

In the UK there are signs that the government is beginning to respond to the movement for pupil voice. For example, a recent White Paper, Schools: Achieving Success (DfES, 2001), stated: 'We will encourage students' active participation in the decisions which affect them about their learning and more widely' (DfES, 2001: 28). However, as Osler suggests, England remains a long way behind some other European countries in terms of its legislative commitment to encouraging pupil participation (Osler, 2001). There is also a need for caution in ensuring that participation is genuine, rather than tokenistic, as Hart points out:

> Tokenism is a particularly difficult issue to deal with because it is often carried out by adults who are strongly concerned with giving children a voice but have not begun to think carefully and self-critically about doing so. The result is that they design projects in which children seem to have a voice but in fact have little or no choice about the subject or the style of communicating it, or no time to formulate their own opinions.
>
> (Hart, 1997: 41)

Another issue that needs to be considered is whether strategies for pupil involvement are being carried out in ways that serve to exclude, or privilege, certain voices. If some pupils find that they are not being listened to, or that their opinions are not taken into account in decision making, then their sense of alienation from school may be heightened. In advocating that schools give attention to the pupil voice we also recognise that these strategies can bring tensions to the surface – and listening to a multitude of voices can present difficult challenges to schools. However, as Lynn Davies points out, reconciling conflicting views is an important aspect of democratic education:

> The importance of pupil voice is not just in engaging [pupils] in the 'delivery' of the formal curriculum, but the crucial message that they can act to influence their immediate world and eventually

perhaps their wider world. This influence has to be tempered by an emphasis on universal rights and responsibilities and by a political literacy which is conducive to analysis and awareness of different forms of 'truth' . . . Genuine promotion of pupil voice is the acceptance and, indeed, encouragement of the positive conflict inherent in a democracy.

(Davies, 2001: 7)

As well as matters of principle there are pragmatic reasons why schools should make the effort to engage all pupils in a dialogue about school improvement. A study by Osler, for example, reports the positive impact that pupil involvement can have on exclusion rates: 'We found that schools which had successfully reduced exclusions had involved students as well as parents in discussing good behaviour and discipline' (Osler, 2001: 3). Indeed, as Paul Cooper points out, it is vital that schools recognise the value in listening to a diversity of pupil voices:

One thing that has been made clear by researchers over the past thirty years is that school pupils (and often those considered to be disaffected, maladjusted or otherwise deviant) are astute and insightful critics of schools and schooling . . . We ignore their insights to the detriment of our schools, the future of our pupils and the future of our society.

(Cooper, 1996: 206)

Our own experience of researching pupils' perspectives leads us to agree wholeheartedly with Cooper's assertion.

In answer to our original question – what's in it for schools? – we would suggest that the pupil voice offers a different path for the future development of education. The growth of interest in listening to what young people have to say, both within schools and outside, bodes well perhaps but we must be wary of the 'bandwagon' appeal (Rudduck and Flutter, forthcoming) that can turn a new development into a short-lived 'flavour of the month'. The transformative potential of pupil participation will be lost if established structures within schools prevent this movement from taking root and flourishing. There is clear evidence that the political and social climate has begun to warm to the principle of involving children and young people but we must wait to see whether schools will provide the right conditions for pupil voice to grow. In 1991 Michael Fullan asked 'What would happen if we treated the student as someone whose opinion mattered?' (1991: 170). We are now, thirteen years later, in a better position to answer his question.

Appendix 1 Guidelines on interviewing pupils

These are some recommendations offering guidance for practitioners who wish to interview their pupils as part of a consultation strategy. For more detailed information about using interview techniques to gather data please see the Recommended Readings section.

The dos

Do try out your interview questions first on a 'pilot' sample (with pupils of a similar age who will not be involved in the actual research) so that you know your questions will be understood and will be likely to prompt useful responses.

Do tell interviewees about your research and why you are interviewing them and what will happen to the data gathered. It is important to assure them that anything they say will be treated confidentially and give them the right to decline to be interviewed. If you are tape-recording the interview, explain why you are doing this and what will happen to the tape after the interview (ensure that anyone transcribing the tape will also preserve the confidentiality of the data).

Do keep careful notes of interviewees' names, ages, gender, form groups and always label tapes carefully. It is also useful to make notes immediately after the interview to give details of any interesting but inaudible aspects of the interview.

Do chat to your interviewees for a few moments before the interview to help them to feel relaxed and comfortable.

Do make use of prompts (photographs, cards with quotes on, objects) to help focus interviewees' ideas.

Do check on anything that is unclear or inaudible – voices often drop when someone is saying something personal or particularly important or when they are trying to express a complex idea or opinion. If necessary, refer the statement back to interviewees and ask them to clarify what they have said, for example, by saying something along the lines of 'I think you said this . . . ? Have I understood what you meant?'

The don'ts

Don't influence your interviewees' answers by giving judgemental responses such as: 'That's a good answer'; 'I agree'; 'You're right', or even by facial expressions expressing surprise or boredom. It is a good idea, however, to use add-on phrases like: 'Could you tell me a bit more about that?'; 'Why do you think that is so?'; 'Would you say that is always the case?'

Don't allow one interviewee to dominate a group interview and encourage others to give their own views in response to what has been said by one pupil. Again, useful follow-up questions could be used, such as: 'Does anyone have a different view on that?' or 'Would you agree with what [name] says?'

Don't stick to your interview questions too rigidly (unless the research is designed systematically to compare responses across individuals or groups) but be ready to follow up an interesting line of conversation if it is related to the issues you're interested in. However, try not to let things wander too far from the subject!

Don't allow too much cross-talk between interviewees so that voices overlap and cannot be heard clearly, and remind the interviewees to try to speak one at a time.

Don't rush interviewees to answer a question. Always give them a few moments to think and reassure them that it is fine to pause.

Don't permit interviewees to name teachers or other students they are talking about who are not present in the interview. If this happens, remind the interviewee(s) that they should not name others and say the name will be deleted from transcripts.

Don't make interviews too long: allow around 20 minutes for a one-to-one interview and 30 to 40 minutes for a group interview.

Appendix 2   Guidelines on using questionnaires

These notes are intended to offer some guidance on things to consider in preparing questionnaires for use in pupil consultation strategies: more detailed information can be obtained in publications referred to in the Recommended Readings section.

The dos

Do carry out a 'pilot' questionnaire with a group of pupils of a similar age to your sample but who will not be taking part in the actual research. This allows you to check whether the questions are clearly understood by the pupils.

Do consider the layout of your questionnaire carefully, making instructions clear and concise and allowing adequate space for pupils to give their responses.

Do ensure that the data is kept confidential where personal information is being given.

Do make sure that you have asked pupils to give all relevant information about themselves: their name [if appropriate]; year or form group; gender; which set(s) they are in and so on. If you are considering levels of attainment as a variable then you or the teacher will need to add this information based on the relevant criteria.

Do allow pupils to have their say: if you are using 'closed' type questions then it is a good idea to give a space at the end of the questionnaire for pupils to express their ideas more fully on the issues that they are being consulted about.

The don'ts

Don't make questionnaires too long as pupils are likely to become bored with giving considered answers and are likely just to tick boxes or give short responses.

If you are using closed answer formats **don't** offer a middle response. For example: *How good do you think the present library resources are? (Please grade from 1 – very good to 5 – very poor).* It is difficult to analyse the responses to a question framed in this way: pupils who give a grade of '3' may mean they consider library resources are adequate or in-adequate or they might simply be opting for the middle grade because they do not use library resources.

Don't allow pupils to influence one another's answers but try to ensure that each questionnaire is completed individually. Where a pupil has some difficulty in completing a questionnaire – for example, if they have poor writing skills – a learning support assistant or older pupil can be asked to help.

Don't use complicated phrases when compiling questions to ensure that pupils will easily understand what is being asked and so that pupils with more limited language skills will also be able to express their thoughts and opinions.

Appendix 3　The research projects

The data presented in this book are drawn from a number of research projects undertaken since 1990 involving members of our research team who have been based mainly at Homerton College and the Faculty of Education, University of Cambridge.

About the projects

An early project on pupils' perspectives on teaching and learning was the longitudinal study of secondary school pupils' perspectives, Making Your Way Through Secondary School (1990–94, directed by Jean Rudduck, University of Sheffield, with Susan Harris, University of Sheffield, and Gwen Wallace, University of Derby and, originally, David Gillborn and Jon Nixon; Julia Flutter (then Day) joined the team in 1994) which was part of the ESRC Research Programme, Innovation and Change in Education. The Making Your Way study was a four-year investigation that aimed to identify aspects of school-work and school life influencing pupils' commitment to learning and their sense of self-as-learner. The research team[1] worked with three comprehensive schools, each with its own particular ethos and reflecting different social contexts, and located in different local education authorities. In each school about thirty Year 8 pupils were tracked through to the end of Year 11. A research team member interviewed

[1] An account of this project is given in: Rudduck, J., Chaplain, R. and Wallace, G. (1995) *School Improvement: What Can Pupils Tell Us?* London: David Fulton.

each pupil once a term and, in addition, the form and year tutors, members of the senior management teams and some subject teachers were interviewed. All interviews were tape-recorded and transcribed and the data were subsequently analysed using a qualitative framework. The project's main findings are outlined below.

Making Your Way Through Secondary School: Pupils' Experiences of Teaching and Learning – a summary of the main findings

Pupils' commitment to learning and their confidence as learners is significantly affected by the conditions of learning they experience

In a context where some pupils are advantaged and some disadvantaged by social background factors, the conditions of learning are an important factor in equalising opportunity. The dimensions of experience that reflect positive conditions of learning are these:

- *respect* for pupils as individuals and as a significant body within the institution of the school
- *fairness* to all pupils, irrespective of class, gender, ethnicity or academic status within the school
- *autonomy* – as a right and a responsibility, and in recognition of physical and social maturity
- *intellectual challenge* that helps pupils experience learning as a dynamic, engaging activity
- *support* in relation to both academic and personal concerns
- *security* in relation to both the physical setting of the school and interpersonal encounters (and reflecting the importance of confidence and self-esteem).

Many pupils experience tension and pressure as they struggle to reconcile the demands of schoolwork with the demands of their personal and social development

If all pupils are to achieve, it is necessary to challenge two commonly held views:

- that the 'important' learning does not begin until Year 10
- that a two-year span of work in Years 10 and 11 means that the pace can be fairly relaxed.

A series of follow-on studies has pursued some of the key issues identified in this initial, large-scale project and the research team has continued to investigate pupils' perspectives on teaching and learning, focusing on a wider range of ages and exploring a range of different aspects of pupils' experiences in school. The format of these investigations has varied: in some projects we have supported teachers in developing pupil consultation to examine issues they are concerned about and in others we have examined specific issues that have been identified as important through our research, or that we have been requested to focus on by outside agencies who are interested in gaining pupils' perspectives on teaching and learning (these agencies have included the Nuffield Foundation, OFSTED, the Department for Education and Skills and various local education authorities). Some of these satellite projects are listed in the summary below (Table A3.1).

The research presented in this book has largely been carried out as part of the Economic and Social Research Council's Teaching and

Table A3.1 Research on pupil consultation: recent projects

Project	Focus
The Effective Learning Project – Thinking about Learning, Talking about Learning, supported by Cambridgeshire LEA Researchers: Julia Flutter, Ruth Kershner, Jean Rudduck, with Paul Cooper, Tim Everton, Donald McIntyre, Pam Pointon, Isobel Urquhart (University of Cambridge) and Cambridgeshire LEA School Inspectors Janet Ardavan, Maggie Holling, Kate Oswald and Paul Overton	A project supporting teacher-led research using pupil consultation to explore theme issues (assessment; engagement; the school as a learning environment; pupils helping other pupils in their learning). **Project report**: Flutter, J., Kershner, R. and Rudduck, J. (1996) *Thinking about Learning, Talking about Learning*. Cambridge: Homerton College/Cambridgeshire LEA.

Table A3.1 (cont'd)

Project	Focus
Improving Learning: The Pupils' Agenda, supported by the Nuffield Foundation Researchers: Christine Doddington, Julia Flutter, Jean Rudduck (University of Cambridge), Helen Addams, Michael Johnstone, Margaret Maden (University of Keele)	A two-year, national investigation of how primary and secondary schools are developing strategies for pupil consultation and pupil participation to improve teaching and learning. **Reports**: *Improving Learning – The Pupils' Agenda (a report for primary schools)*, Cambridge: Homerton College; *Improving Learning – The Pupils' Agenda (a report for secondary schools)*, Cambridge: Homerton College.
Sustaining Pupils' Progress at Year 3, supported by OFSTED Researchers: Eve Bearne, Helen Demetriou, Christine Doddington, Julia Flutter (University of Cambridge)	An investigation of factors affecting pupils' progress at Year 3, drawing on pupils' and teachers' perspectives on teaching and learning. Data were gathered in sixteen infant, junior and primary schools in two local education authorities (Cambridgeshire and Essex). **Report**: Doddington, C. and Flutter, J. with Bearne, E. and Demetriou, H. (2002) *Sustaining Pupils' Progress at Year 3*, Cambridge: Faculty of Education, University of Cambridge.
The Challenge of Year 8, supported by Lincolnshire LEA Researchers: Julia Flutter, Jean Rudduck and Elaine Wilson (University of Cambridge)	A project involving teacher-led initiatives aimed at exploring ways of supporting pupils' progress in learning during the early years of secondary schooling. **Report**: Rudduck, J., Flutter, J. and Wilson, E. (1998) *The Challenge of Year 8*, Cambridge: Homerton College.

Learning Research Programme. This programme, coordinated by Professor Andrew Pollard (Faculty of Education, University of Cambridge), originally by Professor Charles Desforges (University of Exeter), is the most extensive educational research initiative undertaken in the United

Kingdom and is funded by the Higher Education Funding Council for England, Department for Education and Skills, Scottish Executive, National Assembly for Wales and Northern Ireland Executive. The programme fosters partnership between practitioners and researchers in undertaking research and ensuring that it has an impact on teaching and learning. Its key objectives are to:

- enhance learning across a range of ages and stages in education, training and lifelong learning
- develop the capability for transforming the knowledge base relevant to learning into effective and efficient teaching and training practices
- enhance the UK capacity for research-based practice in teaching and learning
- promote and extend multidisciplinary and multi-sector research in teaching and learning.

Further information and up-to-date news on the programme's research can be obtained on the TLRP website: www.tlrp.org

The Network Project, Consulting Pupils about Teaching and Learning (coordinated by Professor Jean Rudduck), was one of four projects taking part in Phase 1 of the Teaching and Learning Research Programme. Much of the data included in this book was gathered in schools taking part in this extensive three-year project which was completed in May 2003. The Network Project's six core projects are outlined below.

ESRC/TLRP Network Project: Consulting Pupils about Teaching and Learning – the six core projects

Project 1: How teachers respond to pupil ideas on improving teaching and learning in different subjects. Researchers: Donald McIntyre and David Peddar, Faculty of Education, University of Cambridge

Project 2: Ways of consulting pupils about teaching and learning and evaluating the impact. Researchers: John MacBeath, Kate Myers and Helen Demetriou, Faculty of Education, University of Cambridge

Project 3: Pupil perspectives and participation: starting and sustaining the process. Researchers: Michael Fielding and Sara Bragg, University of Sussex

Project 4: The potential of pupils to act as (co-)researchers into the process of teaching and learning. Researchers: Michael Fielding and Sara Bragg, University of Sussex

Project 5: How the conditions of learning in school and classroom affect the identity and participation of different groups of pupils. Researchers: Madeleine Arnot and Beth Wang, Faculty of Education, University of Cambridge; Diane Reay, King's College, London; with Isobel Urquhart and Julia Flutter, Faculty of Education, University of Cambridge

Project 6: Breaking new ground: innovative school initiatives involving pupil consultation and pupil participation. Researchers: Julia Flutter, Nick Brown, Elaine Wilson and Eve Bearne, Faculty of Education, University of Cambridge

In addition to the six core projects with schools, a meta-study has been carried out, exploring different dimensions of the link between pupil voice and learning through a series of seminars with experts from various fields. The themes covered in the series were: Changing constructions of children and childhood; Developing pupils' language for talking about learning; Pupil voice and democracy.

An important dimension of the Network Project was the opportunity that it offered to teachers, schools and other agencies to become part of an extensive research programme. All Network members were invited to contribute to the core projects' collective experience and to become involved in discussion and dissemination activities including workshops, conferences and the project website.

Each of these six Network research projects has added to our data collection on pupils' perspectives of teaching and learning and we have drawn on some of this extensive dataset (as well as data from other, earlier projects) to focus on the things that pupils have said make a difference to their learning and achievement. It should be noted that where we have not identified individual pupils or schools this is to preserve confidentiality but each extract is labelled, showing the pupil's year group and, in most cases, the pupil's gender.

Recommended readings

On pupil voice

Baginsky, M. and Hannam, D. (1999) *School Councils: The Views of Students and Teachers*, London: National Society for the Prevention of Cruelty to Children.

Cullingford, C. (1991) *The Inner World of the School*, London: Cassell.

Fielding, M. (2001) 'Students as radical agents of change', *Journal of Educational Change* 2: 123–41.

Forum (2001) Special issue on Student Voice, edited by Michael Fielding, 43: 2.

Jelly, M., Fuller, A. and Byers, R. (2000) *Involving Pupils in Practice: Promoting Partnerships with Pupils with Special Educational Needs*, London: David Fulton.

Osler, A. (2000) *Citizenship and Democracy in Schools: Diversity, Identity, Equality*, Stoke-on-Trent: Trentham Books.

Pollard, A. and Triggs, P. with Broadfoot, P., McNess, E. and Osborn, M. (2000) *What Pupils Say: Changing Policy and Practice in Primary Education*, London: Continuum.

Ruddock, J. and Flutter, J. (2004) *Improving Schools, Involving Pupils*, London: Continuum.

Ruddock, J., Chaplain, R. and Wallace, G. (1996) *School Improvement: What Can Pupils Tell Us?*, London: Falmer.

On researching pupils' views

MacBeath, J. (1999) *Schools Must Speak for Themselves: The Case for School Self-evaluation*, London: Routledge.

MacBeath, J. with Schratz, M., Jakobsen, L. and Meuret, D. (2000) *Self-evaluation in European Schools: A Story of Change*, London: Falmer Press.

School Councils UK (2001) *Primary School Councils Toolkit*, London: School Councils UK.

School Councils UK (2001) *Secondary School Councils Toolkit*, London: School Councils UK.

A useful set of guides for practitioner research is available from the Scottish Council for Research in Education which includes the following titles:

Drever, E. (2003) *Using Semi-Structured Interviews in Small-scale Research: A Teacher's Guide* (SCRE Publication No. 129).
Lewis, I. and Munn, P. (1997) *So You Want To Do Research? A Guide for Teachers on How to Formulate Research Questions* (SCRE Publication No. 136).
Munn, P. and Drever, E. (1999) *Using Questionnaires in Small-scale Research: A Teacher's Guide* (SCRE Publication No. 141, revised edition).
Simpson, M. and Tuson, J. (1995) *Using Observations in Small-scale Research: A Beginner's Guide* (SCRE Publication No. 130).

A set of resources based on the ESRC/TLRP Network Project 'Consulting Pupils about Teaching and Learning' is available.

Arnot, M., McIntyre, D., Pedder, D. and Reay, D. (2003) *Consultation in the Classroom: Pupil Perspectives on Teaching and Learning*, Cambridge: Pearson Publishing.
Fielding, M. and Bragg, S. (2003) *Students as Researchers: Making a Difference*, Cambridge: Pearson Publishing.
MacBeath, J., Demetriou, H., Rudduck, J. and Myers, K. (2003) *Consulting Pupils: A Toolkit for Teachers*, Cambridge: Pearson Publishing.

References

Al-Methen, A. E. and Wilkinson, W. J. (1992) 'Perceived causes of failure among secondary school students', *Research in Education*, 48: 26–41.

Apple, M. ([1979] 1990) *Ideology and Curriculum* (second edition), New York and London: Routledge.

Arnot, M., Reay, D. and Wang, B. (2001) 'Pupil consultation and the social conditions of learning'. Paper presented at the Consulting Pupils Network Project Symposium, BERA Annual Conference, University of Leeds, September 2001.

Arnot, M., Gray, J., James, M. and Rudduck, J. (1998) *Recent Research on Gender and Educational Performance*, London: OFSTED.

Assessment Reform Group (1999) *Assessment for Learning. Beyond the Black Box*, Cambridge: School of Education, University of Cambridge.

Baginsky, M. and Hannam, D. (1999) *School Councils: The Views of Students and Teachers*. London: NSPCC.

Bar-Tal, D. (1982) 'Effects of teachers' behaviour on pupils' attributions', in C. Antaki, and C. Brewin (1982) *Attributions and Psychological Change*, London: Academic Press.

Black, P., Harrison, C., Lee, C., Marshall, B. and Wiliam, D. (2002) *Working Inside the Black Box*, London: King's College, London.

Blatchford, P. (1998) *Social Life in School: Pupils' Experience of Breaktime and Recess from 7 to 16 Years*, London: Falmer Press.

Blatchford, P. and Sharp, S. (eds) (1994) *Breaktime and the School: Understanding and Changing Playground Behaviour*, London: Routledge.

Blishen, E. (1967) *The School That I'd Like . . .* , Harmondsworth: Penguin.

Bonnett, M. (1996) ' "New" era values and the teacher–pupil relationship as a form of the poetic', *British Journal of Educational Studies*, 44.1: 27–41.

Borland, M., Laybourn, A., Hill, M. and Brown, J. (1998) *Middle Childhood: The Perspectives of Children and Parents*, London: Jessica Kingsley Publications.

Britton, J. (1969) 'Talking to learn', in D. Barnes (1969) *Language, the Learner and the School*, Penguin Papers in Education, Harmondsworth: Penguin.

Brown, B. B., Eicher, S. A. and Lohr, M. J. (1986) 'The importance of peer group ("crowd") affiliation in adolescence', *Journal of Adolescence*, 9: 73–95.

Bullock, K. and Wikeley, F. (2000) 'Personal Learning Plans: supporting pupil learning', *Topic*, 24: 8.

Butler, R. (1988) 'Enhancing and undermining intrinsic motivation: the effects of task-involving and ego-involving evaluation on interest and performance', *British Journal of Educational Psychology*, 58: 1–14.

Carroll, J. (1963) 'A model of school learning', *Teachers College Record*, 64: 723–33.

Charlton, T. (1996a) 'The voice of the child in school: listening to pupils in classrooms and schools', in R. Davie and D. Galloway (1996) *Listening to Children in Education*, London: David Fulton.

Charlton, T. (1996b) 'Where is control located?', in K. Jones and T. Charlton (eds) (1996) *Overcoming Learning and Behaviour Difficulties: Partnership with Pupils*, London: Routledge.

Coleman, J. C. and Hendry, L. (1990) *The Nature of Adolescence*, London: Routledge.

Cooper, H. and Hyland, R. (2000) (eds) *Children's Perceptions of Learning with Trainee Teachers*, London: Routledge Falmer.

Cooper, H., Nye, B., Charlton, K., Lindsay, J. and Greathouse, S. (1996) 'The effects of summer vacation on achievement test scores: a narrative and meta-analytic review', *Review of Educational Research*, 66.3: 227–68.

Crane, B. (2001) Revolutionising school-based research, *Forum*, 43.2: 54–5.

CSV (Community Service Volunteers) (2002) *The Impact of Citizenship in Schools*, London: CSV.

Cullingford, C. (1991) *The Inner World of the School*, London: Cassell.

Davies, L. (2001) 'Pupil voice and the quality of teaching and learning'. Paper presented at the ESRC/TLRP Network Project Meta Study Seminar 3, 'Pupil Voice and Democracy', Faculty of Education, University of Cambridge, 15 October 2001.

Davies, L. and Kirkpatrick, G. (2000) *The Euridem Project: A Review of Pupil Democracy in Europe*, London: The Children's Rights Alliance.

DfES (Department for Education and Skills) (2001) *Schools: Achieving Success*, Cm 5230, London: The Stationery Office.

Dockrell, J., Lewis, A. and Lindsay, G. (2000) 'Researching children's perspectives: a psychological dimension', in A. Lewis and G. Lindsay (eds) *Researching Childrens' Perspectives*, Buckingham: Open University Press.

Doddington, C. and Flutter, J. (2002) *Sustaining Pupils' Progress at Year 3*, Cambridge: Publications Dept, Faculty of Education, University of Cambridge.

Doddington, C., Rudduck, J. and Flutter, J. (1999) Improving Learning: The Pupils' Agenda (A Report for Primary Schools), Cambridge: Homerton College Publications.

Doran, C. and Cameron, R. J. (1995) 'Learning about learning: metacognitive approaches in the classroom', *Educational Psychology in Practice*, 11.2: 15–23.

Dweck, C. S. (1986) 'Motivational process affecting learning', *American Psychologist* (Special Issue: Psychological Science and Education), 41.10: 1040–8.

Ellis, T. (1984) 'Extending the school year and day', ERIC Clearinghouse on Educational Management, *ERIC Digest* 7: 1–3.

European Commission (2001) A New Impetus for European Youth White Paper COM (2001) 681, Brussells: European Commission.

Fielding, M. (2001) 'Beyond the rhetoric of student voice: new departures or new constraints in the transformation of 21st century schooling?', *Forum*, 43.2: 100–9.

Fullan, M. (1991) *The New Meaning of Educational Change*, New York, NY: Teachers' College Press.

Galton, M., Hargreaves, L., Comber, C., Wall, D. and Pell, A. (1999) *Inside the Primary Classroom: 20 Years On*, London: Routledge.

Galton, M., Gray, J. and Rudduck, J. (2003) *Progress in the Middle Years of Schooling (7–14): Continuities and Discontinuities in Learning*, Final Report to the DfES in the Transition and Transfer Project, London: DfES.

Gersch, I. (1990) 'The pupil's view', in M. Scherer, I. Gersch and L. Fry (1990) (eds) *Meeting Disruptive Behaviour*, Basingstoke: Macmillan Educational.

Gross, P. A. (1997) *Joint Curriculum Design: Facilitating Learner Ownership and Active Participation in Secondary Classrooms*, Mahwah, NJ: Lawrence Erlbaum Associates.

Hannam, D. (1999) 'Biodiversity or monoculture – the need for alternatives and diversity in the school system'. Paper presented at the conference 'The free child – defining the role and relevance of alternative schools in education today', Summerhill School, UK, 23–26 July 1999.

Hannam, D. (2002) *The Impact of Citizenship in Schools*, London: Community Service Volunteers.

Harris, A. (1996) 'Raising levels of pupil achievement through school improvement', *Support for Learning*, 11.2: 62–7.

Hart, R. A. (1997) *Children's Participation. The Theory and Practice of Involving Young Citizens in Community Development and Environmental Care*, London: Earthscan Publications.

Holloway, S. L. and Valentine, G. (2003) *Cyberkids: Children in the Information Age*, London: RoutledgeFalmer.

James, C. (1968) *Young Lives at Stake*, London: Collins.

James, J., Charlton, T., Leo, E. and Indoe, D. (1992) 'A peer to listen', *Support for Learning*, 6.4: 165–9.

Jarrett, O. S., Maxwell, D. M., Dickerson, C., Hoge, P., Davies, G. and Yetley, A. (1998) 'The impact of recess on classroom behaviour: group effects and individual differences', *Journal of Educational Research*, 92.2: 121–6.

Jelly, M., Fuller, A. and Byers, R. (2000) *Involving Pupils in Practice: Promoting Partnerships with Pupils with Special Educational Needs*, London: David Fulton.

Karweit, N. (1982) *Time on Task: A Research Review*, Report 332, Baltimore, MD and Washington DC: Center for Social Organization of Schools, Johns Hopkins University and National Commission on Excellence in Education.

Kerr, D., Lines, A., Blenkinsop, S. and Schagen, I. (2002) *Citizenship and Education at Age 14: A Summary of the International Findings and Preliminary Results for England*, London: National Foundation for Educational Research/DfES.

Kirby, P. (2001) 'Participatory research in schools', *Forum*, 43.2: 74–7.

Lansdown, G. (1995) *Taking Part: Children's Participation in Decision Making*, London: Institute for Public Policy Research.

Lloyd-Smith, M. and Tarr, J. (2000) 'Researching children's perspectives: a sociological dimension', in A. Lewis and G. Lindsay (eds) *Researching Childrens' Perspectives*, Buckingham: Open University Press.

MacBeath, J. and McGlynn, A. (2003) *Self-evaluation: What's In It for Schools?*, London: Routledge Falmer.

MacBeath, J., Myers, K. and Demetriou, H. (2001) 'Supporting teachers in consulting pupils about aspects of teaching and learning, and evaluating impact', *Forum*, 43.2: 78–82.

McCallum, B., Hargreaves, E. and Gipps, C. (2000) 'Learning: the pupil's voice', *Cambridge Journal of Education*, 30.2: 275–89.

McLaughlin, C., Carnell, M. and Blount, L. (1999) 'Children as teachers: listening to children in education', in P. Milner and B. Carolin (eds) *Time to Listen to Children*, London: Routledge.

National Children's Bureau (NCB) (1998) *Young Opinions, Great Ideas*, London: NCB.

Nieto, S. (1994) 'Lessons from students on creating a chance to dream', *Harvard Educational Review*, 64: 392–426.

Nisbet, J. and Schucksmith, J. (1986) *Learning Strategies*, London: Routledge and Kegan Paul.

Nixon, J., Martin, J., McKeown, P. and Ranson, S. (1996) *Encouraging Learning: Towards a Theory of the Learning School*, Buckingham: Open University Press.

OFSTED (1997) *Tany's Dell Primary School Inspection Report* (ref. no. 114939), London: OFSTED.

OFSTED (1999) *Sandringham School Inspection Report* (ref. no. 117548), London: OFSTED.

OFSTED (2001a) *Falmer High School Inspection Report* (ref. no. 114583), London: OFSTED.

OFSTED (2001b) The Sweyne Park Inspection Report (ref. no. 230985), London: OFSTED.

Osborne, J. and Collins, S. (2001) 'Pupils' views of the role and value of the science curriculum: a focus-group study', *International Journal of Science Education*, 23.5: 441–67.

Osler, A. (2001) 'Student voice, democracy and learning environments'. Paper presented at the ESRC/TLRP Network Project Meta Study Seminar 'Pupil Voice and Democracy', Faculty of Education, University of Cambridge, 15 October 2001.

Parkinson, J. *et al.* (1998) 'Pupils' attitudes to science in Key Stage 3 of the National Curriculum: a study of pupils in South Wales', *Research in Science and Technological Education*, 16.2: 165–76.

Pell, A. and Jarvis, T. (2001) 'Developing attitude to science scales for use with children of ages from five to eleven years', *International Journal of Science Education*, 23.8: 847–62.

Pellegrini, A. D. (1995) *School Recess and Playground Behaviour*, Albany, NY: State University of New York.

Pollard, A. and Triggs, P. with Broadfoot, P., McNess, E. and Osborn, M. (2000) *What Pupils Say: Changing Policy and Practice in Primary Education*, London: Continuum.

Pramling, I. (1990) *Learning to Learn: A Study of Swedish Pre-school Children*, New York, NY: Springer-Verlag.

QCA (Qualifications and Curriculum Authority) (2000) *Citizenship at Key Stages 3 and 4: Initial Guidance for Schools*, London: QCA.

Quicke, J. (1994) 'Pupil culture and the curriculum', *Westminster Studies in Education*, 17: 5–18.

Roche, J. (1999) 'Children: rights, participation and citizenship', *Childhood*, 6.4: 475–93.

Roffey, S., Tarrant, T. and Majors, J. (1994) *Young Friends: Schools and Friendship*, London: Cassell.

Roller, J. (1999) 'Facilitating pupil involvement in assessment, planning and review processes', *Educational Psychology in Practice*, 13.4: 266–76.

Rowe, M. B. (1972) 'Wait-time and rewards as instructional variables: their influence in language, logic and fate control'. Paper presented at the National Association for Research in Science Teaching, Chicago, IL, April 1972.

Rudduck, J. and Flutter, J. (forthcoming) *Improving Schools, Involving Pupils*, London: Continuum Press.

Rudduck, J., Chaplain, R. and Wallace, G. (1996) *School Improvement: What Can Pupils Tell Us?*, London: David Fulton.

Rudduck, J., Flutter, J. and Wilson, E. (1998) *The Challenge of Year 8*, Cambridge: Homerton College/Lincolnshire LEA.

Rutter, M. and Madge, N. (1976) *Cycles of Disadvantage*, London: Heinemann.

Ryan, C. (1976) *The Open Partnership: Equality in Running the Schools*, New York, NY: McGraw-Hill.

Sarason, S. B. (1991) *The Predictable Failure of Educational Reform*, San Francisco, CA: Jossey-Bass.

Schemm, A. and the CBC Research Group (2000) Enhancing Adolescent Engagement in Learning and Decision-Making. Published on the Internet: www.tc.unl.edu/tci/pdf/Enhancing.PDF

Schweinhart, L. J., Barnes, H. V. and Weikart, D. P. (1993) *Significant Benefits: The High/Scope Perry Preschool Study through Age 27*. (Monographs of the High/Scope Educational Research Foundation, 10.) Ypsilanti, MI: High/Scope Press.

Sharp, S., Sellars, A. and Cowie, H. (1994) 'Time to listen: setting up a peer counselling service to tackle the problem of bullying in school', *Pastoral Care in Education*, 12.2: 3–6.

Shorter Oxford English Dictionary (1973), Oxford: Oxford University Press.

SooHoo, S. (1993) 'Students as partners in research and restructuring schools', *The Educational Forum*, 57: 386–392.

Stahl, R. J. (1990) *Using 'Think-time' Behaviours to Promote Students' Information Processing, Learning, and On-task Participation. An Instructional Model*, Tempe, AZ: Arizona State University.

Stahl, R. J. (1994) 'Using "think-time" and "wait-time" skillfully in the classroom', *ERIC Digest*, Abstract no. ED370885, 1–4.

Thomas, W. I. and Thomas, D. S. (1928) *The Child in America*, New York, NY: Alfred P. Knopf.

Valencia, S. W. and Bradley, S. (1998) 'Engaging students in self-reflection and self-evaluation', in S. W. Valencia (ed.) *Literacy Portfolios in Action*, Orlando, FL: Harcourt Brace.

Wade, B. and Moore, M. (1993) *Experiencing Special Education: What Young People with Special Educational Needs Can Tell Us*, Buckingham: Open University Press.

Wade, H., Lawton, A. and Stevenson, M. (2001) *Hear by Right: Setting Standards for the Active Involvement of Young People in Democracy*, Leicester/London: National Youth Agency/Local Government Association.

Warsley, P. A., Hampel, R. L. and Clark, R. W. (1997) *Kids and School Reform*, San Francisco, CA: Jossey-Bass.

Watkins, C. (2001) *Learning about Learning Enhances Performance*, London: University of London Institute of Education School Improvement Network (Research Matters Series No. 13).

Watson, N. and Fullan, M. (1992) 'Beyond school–district–university partnerships', in M. Fullan and A. Hargreaves (eds) *Teacher Development and Educational Change*, Lewes: Falmer Press.

Wheatcroft Primary School Pupils (2001) 'Working as a team: children and teachers learning from each other', *Forum*, 43.2: 51–3.

Wyness, M. (2001) 'Children's space and interests: constructing an agenda for student voice'. Paper presented at the ESRC/TLRP Network Project Meta Study Seminar, 'Pupil Voice and Democracy', Faculty of Education, University of Cambridge, 15 October 2001.

Index